# *ORDEAL*

# *ORDEAL*

---

### *Linda Lovelace*
with Mike McGrady

CITADEL PRESS
Kensington Publishing Corp.
www.kensingtonbooks.com

CITADEL PRESS BOOKS are published by

Kensington Publishing Corp.
850 Third Avenue
New York, NY 10022

All Kensington titles, imprints, and distributed lines are available at
special quantity discounts for bulk purchases for sales promotions,
premiums, fund-raising, educational, or institutional use. Special book
excerpts or customized printings can also be created to fit specific
needs. For details, write or phone the office of the Kensington special
sales manager: Kensington Publishing Corp., 850 Third Avenue,
New York, NY 10022, attn: Special Sales Department;
phone 1-800-221-2647.

First hardcover printing: January 1980
First printing of this trade paperback edition: January 2006

10 9 8 7 6 5 4

Printed in the United States of America

Library of Congress Control Number: 79-23323

ISBN 0-8065-2774-9

## *note*

---

Many of the names in this book have been changed to protect
bystanders The following names have *not* been changed:
Chuck Traynor, Leonard Campagna (a.k.a. Lenny Camp),
Philip J. Mandina, Xaviera Hollander, Bob Wolf, Gerard
Damiano, Harry Reems, Lou Peraino (a.k.a. Lou Perry),
Vinnie, Tony Peraino, Michelle, Al Goldstein, Jim Buckley,
Sammy Davis, Jr., Andrea True, Hugh Hefner, David Winters,
Mel Mandel, Marilyn Chambers, Rex Harrison, Arthur Marks.

# *foreword*

Twenty-five years have passed since the controversial 1980 publication of *Ordeal*. For Linda Lovelace this period was hardly less of a roller coaster ride than the preceding years, and it was to end only after her life came tragically, even eerily, full circle.

With two children and with a husband struggling to get a drywall business off the ground, the 1980s found Linda speaking out against the evils of pornography on behalf of the feminist movement, culminating in her 1986 testimony before the Meese Commission on Pornography. The same year saw publication of her second autobiography, *Out of Bondage* (introduction by Gloria Steinem) and a series of health catastrophes. During a double mastectomy, necessitated by complications from silicone injections more than a decade earlier, it was discovered that her liver was on the verge of collapse due to a severe case of hepatitis C contracted from a blood transfusion after her 1970 car accident. A successful organ transplant followed, but so did a lifelong dependence on expensive anti-rejection drugs.

The ensuing years brought more travail and controversy. After the failure of her husband's business, the family moved from Long Island, New York, to Denver, where Linda worked a variety of jobs before embarking on a new round of anti-pornography lectures. The mid-nineties saw Ron Howard buy film rights to *Ordeal* and a divorce finalized between Linda and Larry Marchiano (on grounds that he was a physically and emotionally abusive alcoholic husband and father), while the new millennium began with a pictorial for the adult magazine *Leg Show*. Explaining what appeared to be an ideological about-face, Linda asserted that "there's nothing wrong with looking sexy as long as it's done with taste."

Having become a grandmother in 1998, Linda spent her last few years living alone and working a series of day and night jobs. On April 3, 2002, Linda sustained severe injuries when her SUV rolled over. On April 22, surrounded by her two children and Larry Marchiano, she was taken off life support. Lost on no one was the coincidence that it was also an auto accident that began her life as Linda Lovelace.

As a coda to the Linda Lovelace story, 2005 saw the hit release of the documentary *Inside Deep Throat*, which looked back at the heady days surrounding the release of *Deep Throat* and revealed just how far the porn industry had come. But perhaps most poignantly, it gave the world one last chance to commune with the woman who was at the center of it all.

# *one*

---

My name is not Linda Lovelace. Not these days. Linda Lovelace is the name of a woman who was much younger than I am now, much more trusting and naïve and innocent. Linda Lovelace disappeared from sight several years ago. If I had my way, the name Linda Lovelace would have vanished at the same time and neither you nor I would ever hear of it again.

But the world won't let Linda Lovelace rest in peace. Today I still can't go to a supermarket or a bus station or a high school basketball game without the risk—the whispers, the pointed fingers, the stampedes.

I haven't been able to escape Linda Lovelace, but I have been able to make peace with her. I understand her and what happened to her. I've written this book so that others will also understand.

My particular concern is with my three-year-old son, who will someday have to learn that his mother was once this woman named Linda Lovelace. He will surely hear one side of the story, the side that comes with a sneer and a dirty laugh. I want him to know the rest of the story. I want the record set straight. This is for him, and it's the truth, the story of what really happened.

Noon of a white-hot Florida day. Recuperating from a bad automobile accident, I was stretched out, as usual, on a chaise longue parked outside my parents' home near Fort Lauderdale. Betsy, a friend from high school days, had phoned to say she was driving up from Miami to visit me.

Although I was self-conscious about the fresh scars that crisscrossed my body, I was wearing a bikini and, lying there in the noon sun, I must have dozed off. A shadow moved across my face and I opened my eyes. Betsy! Then I saw she wasn't alone. There was a young man with her. Even before he came into focus, I reached for a towel and covered myself up.

"Linda, this is Chuck Traynor," Betsy said. "Chuck's the photographer I told you about."

"Hi," I said. "Give me a minute and I'll put something on."

"Don't go to any trouble for us," the young man said. "We're only staying a few minutes—we've got to be back in Miami by two."

My first impression of Chuck Traynor: He was tall, at least six feet tall. Everybody I ever went with was my height or shorter. I was always afraid of the tall, good-looking guys. Tall guys always seemed to expect other people to do things for them; they were generally hung up on themselves.

Chuck Traynor was wearing blue jeans, an open-collared long-sleeved shirt with the sleeves rolled up, and wrap-around sunglasses that looked like motorcycle goggles. Did I find him attractive? It's particularly hard to be true to my memory here. Okay, he was tall; he was twenty-seven years old; he wasn't too skinny; he had dirty-blond hair and, yes, he seemed attractive to me.

At that moment the most attractive part of Chuck Traynor's personality was parked in the driveway. It was a new Jaguar XKE, burgundy colored, with a black leather interior and top. *That* impressed me. You've got to understand, almost everyone I had ever gone out with was driving daddy-and-mommy's car and here was a man with a brand new Jag, all his own.

The other first impressions also were positive. He was friendly, and he quickly showed that he had money to spend.

"Your girlfriend Betsy is really something," he told me. "I tried to buy her a new dress on the way over here and she wouldn't let me."

I went to another room to change into something less revealing and Betsy joined me. We had been best friends in high school, and now, at the age of twenty-one, we were living near each other and becoming friends all over again. I was there to recuperate from an automobile accident, and she was in Miami working as a topless dancer.

"I told you about Chuck," Betsy said. "He's the one who wanted me to be a model. Listen, Linda, I can tell he's impressed by you, too."

"What kind of modeling?"

"Not nude," she said quickly. "Clothing. Strictly fashion modeling. Would that interest you?"

"I'd be interested."

Interested? I'd have been interested in anything that would take me away from my parents' home. We went downstairs and I poured them each a beer.

"You don't drink?" Chuck asked.

"Can't," I said. "The doctors tell me I can't drink anything for two years. My liver got all banged up in an auto accident."

That didn't tell the half of it. I had been in an Opel Cadet just driving onto Taconic State Parkway in New York, still in second gear, when an old Chrysler came skidding sideways over a small hill and crashed into me. My forehead and face hit the windshield; part of one eye was hanging down, my jaw was broken and my lower front teeth were sticking out through my chin. The steering wheel broke my ribs and lacerated both my spleen and liver. This was followed by a leaking intestine and peritonitis.

All my dreams at the time were smashed up with me. I had been working in a boutique, saving money to open my own shop. I had ordered a car and picked out a little house.

But now it would be months before I could do anything again.

"You poor kid," Chuck said. "Still, I don't guess there's any reason you couldn't have a smoke?"

No reason I could think of. Chuck produced a joint, lit it up and handed it to me. I hadn't smoked pot in a long time. However, even taking a puff in my mother's house scared me. One time when my mother caught me with pot, she had dialed the police to turn me in. She would have done it, too, except my father walked over and hung up the phone.

"Linda, we've got to get back to Miami," Chuck said. "I own a little bar and I've got to be there when the next shift comes on at two o'clock. Why don't you come along for the ride?"

He didn't have to ask twice. The three of us piled into the Jag. Chuck did the driving and Betsy sat next to him on the hump. We shared another joint as we drove along.

It's difficult for me now to admit how impressed I was with Chuck during that first meeting, but I was. The only flaw I noticed: He was missing a finger. However, he wasn't self-conscious about it. He explained to me that he had been working underwater and a snapping turtle had suddenly gotten hungry.

Even that story impressed me. The things he had done! He was a pilot who had worked as a crop-duster and had once owned his own private airline. He was a former Marine who had won the marksmanship award for the entire Marine Corps; his prize had been a date with movie star Natalie Wood. He was into flying and sky-diving and skin-diving—yes, I was impressed.

Chuck's bar, the Vegas Inn, was in North Miami, just across the street from a police station and near a Carvel stand. At first glance, the bar seemed less than imposing—your basic one-story, flat-roofed, rectangular building, not much larger than a two-car garage.

Inside the bar it was extremely dark. We walked in from bright sunlight and it took several moments for my eyes to adjust. The only light came from winking black lights bouncing off day-glo decorations. The customers were construction workers, truck drivers, garage mechanics—just regular guys killing a few hours with the jukebox or the pool table or the barmaid.

"This is nice," I told Betsy.

"Nice?" she said. "It's a dump."

"Well, it's nice to be out," I said. "You don't know how miserable it is back there at home, having to go back and live with my parents all over again. They still treat me like some kind of kid."

"Your mother hasn't changed."

"She's worse than ever," I said. "But I'd rather not talk about her now."

My mother has always been very emotional toward me. When I was four years old, she started beating me—first with a belt, later with the buckle of the belt. She would hit me for the smallest thing. One time she sent me down to the drugstore for nosedrops—Neosynephrine—and I came back with the wrong kind. I was only eleven and she hit me with a broomstick for that mistake. She said I would have gotten the right bottle if I didn't have my mind on boys so much.

*Boys.* That was a laugh. Boys were the last thing on my mind. No one at home ever told me anything about sex. Only one message ever came through clearly: Sex was bad. Once, some of my girlfriends were talking about their parents going to bed to make babies and I tried to picture my parents doing that. No way. One of my friends used the word "fuck" and no one knew what it meant. I said I'd ask my mom and I did: "Hey, mom, what does the word 'fuck' mean?" I got smacked in the face, kicked in the ass, and sent to my room.

When I got my period for the first time, I was sure it was God's punishment for one sin or another. Finally, I told my mother about it. She marched me into the bathroom and pointed to the box of Kotex: "Here. You get it once a month, it lasts about five days, and you wear this."

That was the sum total of my childhood sex education.

"Linda, is something the matter?"

Betsy was shaking my shoulder.

"No," I said, "No, I was just daydreaming. Tell me about your friend Chuck."

"Chuck? Nothing. Nothing's going on."

"Really?"

"Believe it," she said. "He's a nice guy, but he's just a friend. Seriously. I've slept over at his house a couple of times, and he didn't even come on to me."

We were joined by one of Chuck's friends, Benny. Benny was a regular hillbilly, very much into country music, and he had a pleasant personality, not at all loud or crude. He was good-looking, black-haired and muscular from construction work. I suddenly realized that this was my first time out in many months and it felt good. I drank a Coke with Benny and later accepted his offer of a date.

It had been a year since my last date and even before that, my life had been very sheltered. I had no boyfriends until high school. Then, although I dated sometimes and would kiss a boy, I would not go any farther than that. I wouldn't neck. I was known as Miss Holy-Holy and for a time even wanted to be a nun.

I can think of almost every guy who ever asked me out; they hardly ever asked me out a second time. As I got older, the boys became more persistent. Whenever I found a boy who wouldn't hassle me, it was beautiful. I was the kind of girl who liked to go down by the ocean and hold hands. I still am.

I don't want to pretend that I was always Miss Holy-Holy. I fell in love once or twice; I lost my virginity at age nineteen, and when I was twenty, I gave birth to an illegitimate child that my mother put out for adoption.

Anyway, Benny was my first date in many months and during the next few weeks, the four of us got together several times. Benny would pick me up at home and the four of us would go to Chuck's house where we'd smoke pot and talk. It was nice to have some social life again.

But Benny was not going to be the man in my life—not

for long anyway. Chuck and Betsy had stopped seeing each other and then Chuck began coming on to me. I'd be with Benny at the bar, and I'd suddenly notice Chuck was looking over at me, smiling. I would avoid looking back at him —I was too shy for that—but I was interested.

Then one day, after I had known Benny for six weeks, I came into the bar and I heard the barmaid talking about him: "Oh, Benny had another big fight with his wife and this time she took out after him with a gun."

His *wife!* I had gone out with Benny all that time and somehow he had neglected to mention a wife. That blew my head. I have always had great respect for marriage and would never have done anything to hurt one. I could never take a responsibility like that. I spoke to Benny just once or twice more. He tried to convince me that it was over with his wife, that they were getting a divorce, but by then it was too late.

The next week, when Chuck asked me out, I went with him.

# *two*

---

I started seeing Chuck. He would drive all the way to my parents' home in the middle of the day, and we'd take off together.

"Where are we going today?" I'd ask.

"Oh, I heard about a new little shop down off the Palmetto Expressway," he'd say. "I think we'll go down there and see if they have anything pretty enough for you."

I liked that kind of thing. Other guys I knew might buy a present at Christmas or on my birthday, but they didn't ever take me out just to buy something pretty to wear.

I still didn't know how to accept a gift from a man and often I'd turn it around. We'd go out shopping together and I'd pick out something nice for him. He loved those loose-fitting Indian shirts that you could find in head shops. Money was no object. He flashed it around freely, and he didn't mind spending it.

Chuck was behaving like a gentleman with me. Lighting my cigarettes, opening car doors, listening to what I said. While he was very mellow with me, he had an air of authority in dealing with other people. He was always in control of the situation. No one ever pushed him around. He never came on to me sexually at all.

Most days I went with him to his bar while he counted out the register and took care of business. Nights we went to the movies or watched television. He liked war movies the most. One of his favorites was *Tora! Tora! Tora!,* a movie I couldn't stand because of all the people getting shot up.

My mother went on treating me like a kid. As we'd leave, she'd say, "Be sure to be home by eleven o'clock." When you're twenty-one years old, you don't want to be told to be home at eleven o'clock. You also don't want to hear, "Where are you going?" and "Who are you meeting?" and "Be sure to call me when you get there so I'll know where you are."

My family was really something. I'd see those families on television, sitting around a table, discussing things—actually talking with each other—but my parents were never like that. At the dinner table, my mother would complain about what happened to her all day—what this one did to her, what that one did to her—and every now and then my father would say, "Yep."

When I was young, I'd hear my father come home from work late at night. He had been a policeman. Often he would stop at a bar on the way home from work and then he'd come home drunk. I can remember one night when my mother attacked him with a butcher knife. She was scream-ing—and when she screams, she really hits high C—and I was sitting at the top of the stairs, praying that it would stop. I never saw the two of them kiss or even hold hands.

Now, at age twenty-one, I was back with them. Nothing had changed except the address. The new address was a retirement town fifteen or twenty miles west of Ford Lauder-dale, where you drove through a pair of arches and found yourself in the middle of nowhere. A post office, a Seven-Eleven, a bunch of $50,000 homes built around a golf course.

My father had retired from the police force and was now working as a security guard for an airline. My mother worked as a waitress at a local golf club. When she wasn't working, she spent much of her time worrying about my getting home by eleven o'clock.

She was serious about that, dead serious. If I was just fifteen minutes late, she'd greet me at the door with a hard slap across the face or a rap with a broomstick. My father managed never to be around to see this. The one time he walked into the room while she was hitting me, he turned on his heels and went the other way. When I was sixteen, my father had told me we'd just have to take my mother's behavior in stride: "Your mother's going through change of life." Well, that change of life had become her way of life.

One night my mother really let me have it. It was the last time she ever hit me, and the last time she ever will hit me. The next day I was quiet and moody and Chuck guessed what had gone down.

"Mothers never realize that their little girls grow up," he said.

"You know what kills me the most?" I said. "That's when I'm watching television and I see some kind of show like *Father Knows Best*. That kind of family. Whoever had a family like that?"

"That's just television," Chuck said. "But you don't have to put up with your folks any more. You're a big girl now."

"I wish I had a choice."

"You do," Chuck said. "Here's what you do—you pack up your stuff and you move in with me."

"I couldn't do that," I said. "But I've got to get away from my mother."

"You could do it," Chuck said. "At least think about it. I'm serious."

I did think about it. I thought about nothing else all the while Chuck was driving us south toward Coral Gables. There was no real reason *not* to go with him. It would be a chance to be free, to come and go as I pleased.

But what did I really know about Chuck? At that time I didn't know that he had a police record, that he'd been found guilty of assault and battery. I didn't know that he was facing charges for smuggling drugs into this country. I didn't know that he had run a house of prostitution. I didn't know that he would one day brag to me about the people he had killed. I only knew one thing: He was giving me a chance to get away from my parents.

Chuck was pulling up in front of Worth Devore's apartment in Coral Gables. This meant just one thing: Chuck was running low on pot. Whenever he started to run out of marijuana, it was time to visit Worth. Worth was a pilot for a private company and he flew all over the world; he had a beautiful apartment decorated with African artifacts; he had a new Camaro; he had plenty of money, and he had an apparently endless supply of Colombian pot.

The two of them looked over some weavings that Worth had just brought back with him, then Chuck turned to me.

"Linda, why don't you just make up your mind and do it. You could move in with me tonight."

"I'll do it," I said. "I've got to get away from my folks . . . except I hate the thought of calling them. What can I say to them?"

"Nothing," Chuck said. "Why bother to call them at all?"

"I've got to. I've got to tell them something."

"Don't call them tonight." His voice took on a sharpness I hadn't heard before. "They'll just con you into coming home, and you don't want that."

"You don't know my mother. If I don't call, she'll have every cop in town out looking for me."

"The only place they'd look for you is my place," Chuck said. "But we'll be spending the night right here with Worth. If that's okay with you, Worth."

"Help yourself," Worth said. "You guys can have my room, and I'll take the couch."

We were in the bedroom then, sitting on the edge of Worth's bed, but the argument was still going on inside of me. I should call, I shouldn't call. . . .

"You don't have to call." Chuck's voice had taken on a soothing quality by this time. "I'm telling you, you speak to them tonight and you're letting yourself in for all kinds of aggravation."

I was crying then, really letting out the blues, and Chuck gave me a shoulder to lean against. I would cry for a while, then stop, then get mad—mad at my mother for being able to have this kind of effect on me. Chuck was very gentle with me. He seemed to know what I was going through and just what to say. He seemed to have only my welfare at heart. Worth was playing Beethoven on his stereo in the other room and the music seemed to float in from some quiet and peaceful world.

This was the first time I had ever taken a stand against my parents, the first time I had done something directly against them. My feelings were all mixed up. One minute it seemed right and then it was wrong; one minute I was strong and then I was weak.

Chuck was being gentle and comforting, stroking my hair, occasionally lighting up a joint and passing it over to me.

"Chuck, I don't know what's the right thing to do."

"Sure you do," he said. "This is the right thing. The right thing is to do nothing."

The argument was settled finally by the clock, by the lateness of the hour. It was too late to go home, then too late to call, finally too late to make sense of anything.

"Let's go to bed," Chuck said. He watched me as I took off my clothes and put them over a chair. I came to bed wearing my bra and panties. "Well, I didn't know I was with a virgin tonight."

"I'm not."

Not a virgin, but still an innocent. I hadn't even thought about making love with Chuck or whether that would be part of the package. It didn't seem all that important. The only thing that seemed important that night was getting away from my parents. I don't know exactly how to explain this, but compared to the drama of leaving home, sex with Chuck seemed like a small thing.

Chuck made love to me that night, but not really. I didn't know what to expect from a man, and I had no way of knowing whether or not there was anything wrong with Chuck. I realize now that he couldn't achieve a full erection.

"Don't worry about anything," he told me. "I'll be taking care of you from now on."

I guess that was what I wanted to hear more than anything else. While he was trying to make love to me, there was no talk about love or anything of that sort. But he did say he would take care of me. And then he said something that really surprised me.

"Linda, why don't you suck me?"

"I can't do that."

Then he tried something else. I didn't know then what he was trying, but I didn't let that happen either. I now know that he was trying to go down on me, but at that time it just seemed weird. In a few minutes he was finished.

You have to remember, I was not Linda Lovelace then. I was Linda Boreman, the daughter of a policeman. I was Linda Boreman who was raised in Yonkers, New York, and attended Catholic schools—St. John the Baptist in Yonkers and Maria Regina High School in Hartsdale. During grade school my ambition was to be a nun. In ninth grade I was elected vice-president of my class and I enjoyed playing basketball more than anything else.

When I was very young, my mother would sometimes ask me what I wanted from life. I never had to think before answering her. I *knew*. When I was twenty-one, I was going to get married and have a family. I was going to have a house that I would keep very clean, and there would be a garden with flowers. That was my whole dream—marrying someone and living happily with a family of my own.

But now I was twenty-one, and I was sharing a bed with a man I didn't love. The few other times I had made love there had always been a nice feeling afterwards. There was no nice feeling this time. Possibly because the act had been done without any real emotion on either his part or mine. Afterwards there was just a question in my mind: Why did I let him do it?

# *three*

---

I slept well that night, extremely well, and would have slept through the next morning except that Chuck woke me early. He explained that he was a chronic early riser and I might as well get used to it. That bit of information made me realize just how little I knew about the man I was planning to live with.

Still, that first morning nothing could dispel my feeling of well being. I wasn't even nervous when I telephoned my father at work.

"Where've you been, Linda?" he said. "Your mother's been—"

"I know," I said. "I'm with Chuck. I'm going to be staying with Chuck for a while. I can't come home anymore."

"Your mother's going to be very upset."

My father wasn't at all disturbed, but that didn't surprise me. He never reacts to things. He's a perfect Aquarius; you could put him in the middle of an earthquake and he'd go right on doing whatever he had been doing.

"Dad, I'm going to have to get some of my clothes," I said. "I'd like to come by when Mom's at work."

"I just hope you know what you're doing."

"I do. Don't worry."

"Well, Linda, just be careful."

"I will."

"Your mother's sure going to be mad," he said. "You're leaving me with some mess on my hands."

"Good-bye, Dad."

Chuck had been listening to the entire conversation and now he was smiling.

"Congratulations," he said. "You handled that very well."

I thought so, too. Those first feelings of freedom were wonderful while they lasted. It's odd, but I look back at that moment now and my memory reads Chuck's smile in a different way. Then I thought he was sharing my joy. Now, I realize that I had just lived up to his fondest expectations; I had just taken that first blind step into his trap.

Not that it seemed like a trap at first. It seemed anything but. That first day, even before we got back to his place, Chuck took me out and bought me a couple of new blouses and a change of underwear. Those first few days were days of incredible freedom. Being able to come in later than eleven o'clock at night and not get smacked across the face—what a luxury!

Life became a day-to-day affair, casual and unplanned. The simple pleasure of being away from my parents was enough; there was no need to think beyond the moment. In my mind there was some vague picture of returning to New York and getting back into the boutique business—but this was just a daydream, and there are no schedules in daydreams. Whenever I thought about actually going out and getting a job, Chuck was there to dissuade me.

"You don't worry about that, not yet," he said. "This way we can be together all day. You want a job? I'll tell you what, you can help me out with the bar."

"But I've got to make some money."

"Sure you do, and you will," he said. "But there's more than enough time for that later on. What you should be doing now is just taking it easy."

My new life revolved around the Vegas Inn. The first thing in the morning, after waking up, we'd go down and clean up the bar. Then we'd stop at a fast-food place that specialized in hamburgers and waffles and we'd have one or the other, depending on our mood and the time of day.

Then it was back to the bar to check the beer supply and to make sure all the deliveries had been received. If the bar was running low on wine, we'd go down to the Seven-Eleven store for refills. Then Chuck would get together the start-up money, the right amount of change and bills, put that in the cash register, and check in the barmaid.

In the afternoons we'd drive around, hang out, and stop back at the bar whenever anything needed doing. At night there was always the movies. We practically lived in movie theaters; the movies changed on Sundays and by the time Friday came around, we'd have seen all the new ones.

Somewhere along the line, we'd grab something to eat, watch a little television, doze off, and then wake up in time to close the bar late at night. It was what you might call a relationship. At times Chuck was even complimentary to me. He'd say I was good-looking or he'd say I should be in movies. *Oh, Lord!*

I was getting to know Chuck—but slowly. The information came to me in dribs and drabs. One of the first things I learned was that he liked to eat all of his meals out, generally at fast-food stands. His refrigerator was always empty, except for milk and Coke. During all the time I was with him, I cooked no more than a couple of meals at home.

Chuck wouldn't tell me much about himself so I had to learn from other sources. The way I learned that he was a diabetic was typical. One morning he had a seizure, and I had no idea what was happening. I woke up and he was lying on the floor, gasping and thrashing around. I called an ambulance. Later Chuck told me about the diabetes and what to do if he ever had another attack.

Next I learned that he was facing a big criminal trial. I read about this in the newspapers; a certain Charles (Chuck)

Traynor had been caught carrying away a bale of marijuana that an airplane had dropped in a field south of Miami. At first Chuck told me that he had just stumbled across the stash but later he told me the truth. Whatever Chuck chose to tell me, he was convincing. He could tell me the sky was green and I'd believe him, even though I was looking right up into a blue sky.

Gradually I learned about some of the things that upset him. My smoking, for example. I was up to about two packs a day and every time I lit up, he gave me one of those looks.

"Why don't you just quit?" he asked me.

"I can't."

"Sure you can," he said. "I could help you quit. I've helped dozens of people to quit smoking. By hypnotism. I could hypnotize you out of smoking."

"How do you know you could hypnotize me?"

"Are you kidding?" he said. "You'd be a snap. You wouldn't have to worry about a thing. I learned how to hypnotize people when I was down in Honduras."

"I don't know if I like the idea."

"Then you might as well forget it. It won't work unless you want me to do it, unless you trust me completely. It's just that I hate to see you hurting yourself. Hypnotism could help you in a dozen different ways. You're always saying how tired you are, how you never get enough sleep. You're feeling tired right now, aren't you? Listen to me, Linda, I could put you under right now—just for a few minutes—and when you woke up it'd be like you had eight hours sleep."

He had me lie down on the rug and stare at something bright around his neck while he talked. I don't remember what he said, but in a couple of minutes I was sound asleep. When he snapped me out of it, I was fully rested. All as advertised.

We went through this a half-dozen times before he even started with the cigarettes. He told me that before he could get me to give up cigarettes he had to have my complete trust. Well, he already had me trusting him and a few days later he did, in fact, persuade me to give up cigarettes. I'm not sure whether it was the hypnotism or just that I didn't want Chuck to feel that he had failed. Whatever the reason, I no longer smoked.

Once he had done these two things—gotten me to rest and to give up cigarettes—he started in on something else. It hurts to dredge up some of these old memories, but they're too important a part of the story to ignore. I'm talking about our love life—if "love life" is even the right phrase. It was never much, really, half-hearted attempts maybe once a week, if that.

He kept asking me to take him in my mouth but that was still very difficult for me to do. I wanted to please him, but not that way. He told me that was the only way he could become fully aroused, and I told him that it just made me too uncomfortable. However, my "no" never quite ended a discussion.

"I don't get it," he said. "Why do you make such a big deal out of it? Everyone does it."

"Chuck, you know something? Before I met you, I never even *heard* of that before."

"Well, just touch it then," he said. "See, it's not going to bite you."

"Chuck, please . . ."

"Pet it," he said. "It likes to be petted."

This is very embarrassing to me, embarrassing two ways—both remembering it and putting it down here. He made me feel naive, silly, and dumb for not doing it; then amateurish when I tried to do it. It was a major hurdle for me to just hold it in my hands, and let my mouth get near it. A couple of times he held my head tightly with his hands and forced it into my mouth.

"You know why you don't like it," he said. "It's the gagging mechanism. Well, I can cure you of the gagging mechanism the same way I cured you of cigarette smoking. It's just a conditioned reflex and you can control it. You can learn to relax your throat muscles completely."

"I don't think that's possible."

"Oh, yeah, it is," he said. "That's something I learned in the Orient—there were a lot of chicks there who could swallow it, the whole thing. Their whole philosophy was to completely satisfy their man and they sure knew how to do that."

"Chuck, I don't like the taste."

"I know," he said. "That's the whole thing—that's another reason to learn how to swallow it. If the man is all the way in, you don't taste a thing. In a way, you'd be helping yourself."

"Why do we have to keep talking about this?"

"Because this is what I happen to like," he said. "It all comes down to whether or not you want to make me happy."

"I want you to be happy."

"Well?"

I went along with him. As I say these words, I realize that I went along with too much in those days. But I was sure that all of this was just temporary. I was biding my time, healing my wounds, getting ready to go back up to New York and start a new life. Little did I know that my new life had already started.

Chuck had learned hypnotism in Honduras and he had learned exotic sexual practices from the Japanese. Sometimes I have to wonder what my life would have been like if Chuck Traynor had not been a traveling man.

Still, no one was twisting my arm, not yet. Everything was mild and gradual, one small step and then another. This wasn't something we did—or even talked about—every day. And always Chuck would say that it was "no big deal" or "no big thing." But it was.

Then something else began to happen. It started in such small ways that I didn't see the pattern until much later. When you're very close to something, you see only the fragments, the isolated incidents, not the patterns.

The first thing I noticed was that the bar was suddenly becoming much looser, much more risqué. One night I was there counting out the register—Chuck had turned most of the bookkeeping over to me—when one of the barmaids stripped off her blouse and her brassiere and started serving the drinks topless. She must have been doing this for some time because none of the customers made any comment.

That was the beginning. Sometimes we'd be home late at night, getting ready to go back and close up the bar, and we'd get a call from one of the barmaids telling us not to come over yet. I asked Chuck what was happening and he said not much; the barmaids were just dancing naked for some of the regular customers.

Chuck took delight in passing along information of this nature. He'd throw out some tidbit like that; then he'd study my reaction. I seldom disappointed him because at the time I was easily shocked. My major reaction to all the changes at the bar was to stay away.

"It's just as well you don't go down there so often," Chuck said.

"Why's that?"

"Well, I wouldn't want you hanging around Roxanne," he said. "It turns out that Roxanne's bisexual."

"Really?"

"Yeah, how about that? Could you tell that she was bisexual?"

"I don't know," I said. "What's bisexual?"

"She's into other chicks as well as men," he said. "She's got a girlfriend she goes to bed with."

When Chuck told me something outrageous like that, I never knew whether to believe him. Roxanne couldn't have been much older than seventeen, and she seemed very sweet.

Late one night we went over to close down the bar. From the outside it looked as though it were already closed down. No lights were showing. Inside it was almost completely dark. We couldn't see a thing, but we could hear the music coming from the juke box.

Then I saw Roxanne, the young barmaid. She was totally naked, standing on top of the bar and twisting slowly to the music. While she was dancing, a man at the bar reached up and put something—it looked like a dollar bill—into her vagina. She saw us coming in but she didn't stop dancing.

The second barmaid—this was a very cold girl with black raggedy-looking hair—was lying on top of a table in the back of the room. One of the customers was hunched over on top of her, making love to her with his trousers down around his ankles. A second customer had his thing in her mouth, and a third customer was rubbing her breasts very hard.

Even while I saw this, I couldn't accept it. This went beyond my wildest imagination. The amazing thing was that no one even missed a beat when we walked into the bar. I wheeled around and reached for the door. Chuck grabbed my arm but his eyes never left the action.

"Where you going?" he asked.

"Out of here."

"Okay," he said, "have it your way."

"I don't want to see any more."

"Ah, it's no big thing," he said. "I guess I should've called first."

"Chuck, this is *sick!*"

It wasn't the fact of the sex that upset me; it was the nature of the sex. I couldn't imagine anyone—even prostitutes—doing something so incredibly personal with other people around. That was beyond my reach. It never occurred to me that Chuck might have staged the whole thing for my benefit.

"I guess you're right," he said to me. "I'm going to have to check out these girls a little more closely. They're getting a little out of hand. Too much of that and the cops'll close the place down."

A couple of days later, Chuck had a visit from an old friend named Theresa. Theresa was very sweet, with a pretty heart-shaped face and long black hair. She told me how lucky I was to be living with a wonderful man like Chuck. She said that she had always looked upon Chuck as a big brother. Later Chuck talked with me about Theresa.

"You know, she used to work for me."

"At the bar?"

"No," he said. "That was before I got into the bar business. She used to work for me as—she was a working girl."

"A working girl?"

"A hooker," he said. "She was one of the best prostitutes that ever worked for me."

I was startled by that bit of news. I thought prostitutes always wore fishnet stockings, high heels, too much makeup, and hair teased up to the sky. I was shook-up to learn that Chuck once ran a house of prostitution. This completely decked me.

Chuck began having financial difficulties. He no longer bothered to open the obvious bills and he stopped using credit cards. The telephone disappeared and then the electricity was cut off for a few days.

"The bar's not doing so good," he explained.

As his finances waned, Chuck reminisced more and more about "the good old days" when he ran a string of prostitutes. He talked about what nice girls most of the hookers were, just like Theresa, and how well they had done for him.

"You know what we could do?" he said. "We could start it up again. You could answer the telephones—just make the appointments and we'd get out of hock once and for all."

"I could never do something like that."

"Sure you could," he said. "There's nothing to it. Once you get the hang of it, it's like any other job."

"It would be okay for some people, but not me. If someone else wants to do it, fine. But I just couldn't do it."

"A woman has a product," he said, "and she should use it."

That bothered me. All his talk about prostitutes and starting up a new business didn't bother me as much as that. But he said those same words several times—"A woman has a product and she should use it"—and that was always very offensive to me.

As the money situation worsened, so did Chuck's temper. He never put any money in the bank anymore. He would take the cash from the bar, put it in his pocket and carry it around until it all disappeared. Although I was supposed to be his bookkeeper, Chuck stopped talking to me about money. I understood what was happening. One day we were going to the bar, and the next day there was no bar to go to. One day we were driving a new Jaguar, and the next day we were in an eight-year-old Volkswagen.

"Linda, I've got to start up the old business again and I want you to run it for me."

"I can't!"

"You'd be the madam, nothing more than that."

"What do you mean, 'nothing more than that'?"

"I mean, you'd be arranging things for other chicks, that's all."

"Chuck, I can't. I don't even want to talk about it anymore."

"Maybe you don't want to talk about it," Chuck said, "but you're going to do it. One way or the other."

That was the first of many threats. I began to pick up a new tone in Chuck's voice, then a new phrasing. It started as, "Would you want to?" It became, "This is important to me." And, finally, "You're going to wish you had said yes."

"You can do whatever you want to," I told him. "But I don't want anything to do with it. Just leave me out. The whole business is dirty to me. I can't stand the thought of a girl going to bed with a lot of guys just to get paid for it."

"Linda, this is no big thing," he said. "There'd be nothing to it. I'd call up my old customers and tell them I'm back in business. You won't have anything to do with the men at all. You'd just be on the phone. I'm telling you, there's only one thing you'd be handling and that's a telephone."

"Chuck, don't talk that way. I've been thinking everything over and I know that it's time I got back up to New York and—"

That sentence was never completed. He hit me on the side of the head and everything went bleary. Then I was lying on the floor and he was kicking me with his Frye boots, hurting me in a way that I had never been hurt before. At first, as he was kicking me, he seemed quiet and cold-blooded, very methodical about it. But when I started to scream, he became excited, sexually excited. For the first time, I saw him fully aroused. Somehow the beating concluded with him raping me on the floor. Then he was through with me, and I didn't dare move.

"You're not going anywhere," he said. "You're not fucking going anywhere without me."

The hurting stopped but the fear wouldn't go away. The fear and the questioning. Why me? Why would he come down so hard on me? Why didn't he just use one of his hookers? Now I can guess at the answer; it's because an experienced hooker would have been too smart for him. It's because a streetwalker would not have been stupid and naive and gullible and scared.

# *four*

---

One day it was my home, the next day it was prison. The following morning when the telephone rang, I reached for the receiver and Chuck removed it from my hand. He answered it and then turned to me.

"It's your fucking mother," he said. "Take it on the extension and tell her you don't want her to call anymore."

"Chuck, I'm not going to—"

"I'll tell you what you're not going to do," he said. "And what you're fucking going to do. I'll be listening to every word and you're going to tell her not to call anymore. Tell her you've got nothing more to say to her."

"What're you saying?"

"Do what I tell you," he hissed. "Just fucking do it! If you know what's good, kiss momma goodbye. Kiss her off now or you'll get another sample of last night."

"Hello, Mother," I heard myself say. "Look, I don't want you to call me anymore."

From that moment on, Chuck didn't let me out of his sight. Instead of asking me to do things, he told me. And as if to back up his words, he was always playing with his guns. One was a .45 caliber Walther pistol, an eight-shot automatic that had once belonged to a policeman. Chuck also had a semi-automatic machine gun.

Every day, while he played with his guns, we went through the same sequence. He would tell me he was going to resume his prostitution business and I was going to be his new madam. I would tell him no. He would hit me. Before too long, I learned to keep my opinions to myself. I didn't change them but I no longer bothered expressing them.

My only honest conversations those days were with God. I was praying all the time, praying for help, praying for something to make it all go away, praying for Chuck to slip up and leave me alone for a few minutes. I knew what I would do then—run for my life—the very minute I could get away from him and his Frye boots.

This went on into July, a typical Florida July with the temperature up over ninety degrees every day, the shirt always sticking to your back and never enough air to go around.

"Let's go for a ride."

For a change, Chuck seemed to be in a good mood. He was wearing his yellow-and-black shirt and that was generally a reliable indication that he was feeling all right. Although his Volkswagen had no air conditioning, I was happy to go for the ride. For a few hours I'd be away from the prison.

Chuck never bothered to tell me our destinations and I had learned not to ask. Our conversation, not much to start with, had pretty much come to a stop by this time. Since he was heading south, I assumed we would be going to Worth Devore's house for more pot. But then Chuck took a different turn and pulled up in front of a Holiday Inn in South Miami, a sprawling two-story building not far from the University of Miami.

A sign outside the Holiday Inn advertised a big buffet lunch—all you could eat for $2.95—and that prospect cheered me up. It was lunchtime and I was famished. But Chuck drove past the entrance to the restaurant and stopped at the motel. Now I was curious.

"Where are we going?"

"To see a couple of people," he said.

"Business?"

"Yeah, business."

All that meant to me was no buffet lunch. It also meant that Chuck was going to try to con some businessmen into taking part in one of his scams, probably his new prostitution business, since that was all he ever seemed to talk about anymore.

Well, that didn't concern me and I had resolved that it never would concern me. Maybe it was the sunshiny brightness of the day or just being in a Holiday Inn, but I found myself beginning to relax. For at least a couple of hours I couldn't be beaten or threatened.

We walked down the central corridor of the motel, up one flight of stairs, down another hallway all the way to the end. We stopped at the very last room and Chuck rapped on the door three times. There was a long narrow window beside the door. The curtain jerked to one side and a man's face stared out at us. The curtain fell back into place and the door opened.

There were five men in the room, all businessmen and all distinguished in appearance, at least distinguished in comparison to Chuck's normal associates. They were wearing ties and jackets; their hair was receding or graying; their ages ranged from thirty-five to fifty-five. I couldn't imagine how Chuck was going to be able to con this type of man, but I was much more concerned by my hunger pangs: When were we going to eat?

We were in a large room with twin beds separated by a small table. A second table was near the door, and two of the men were seated there, within easy reach of the room-service setups. Over at the far end of the room there was a combination bathroom-dressing room with a fold-up partition. One of the men greeted Chuck like a long-lost friend.

"Hey, Chuckie, it's been a long time between times."

"Sure has," Chuck said. "Too long."

"Got anything new goin' on?"

"You'll see. This is Linda."

"Well, hel-*lo*, Linda."

The others came over then and introduced themselves. Although they all seemed to be respectable businessmen, they weren't above giving me the old once-over.

"Would you care for something to drink?" one of them asked.

"I don't drink."

"That's very commendable," he said.

"But I wouldn't mind some ginger ale."

"No sooner said than done."

One of the men was the president of a bank, and a second was his chief executive officer. The other three ran small businesses. Although they had all been drinking, they were neither raucous nor loud.

Chuck was busy talking with the bank president when I excused myself to go to the bathroom. I found it slightly odd that Chuck hadn't yet come to the point. We had been in the room a quarter of an hour and I still had no idea what Chuck was trying to sell. Well, there was no rush. The air-conditioned room had cooled me off nicely and I was finally feeling comfortable.

When I came out of the bathroom, the partition separating the dressing room and the rest of the room had been closed. Chuck was waiting for me and there was a look on his face that I hadn't seen before. It was a sneer—no, more intense than a sneer.

"You know those five guys out there," he said.

"Well—"

"You're going to fuck all five of them."

"Chuck, don't talk crazy."

"Oh, you're gonna fucking do it all right," Chuck said. "Believe me, you're gonna do it. I've *promised* these men. I've given my word. You tell me you don't want to run my business. I give you every chance in the world and you tell me no. Okay. You don't want to run it, then you can be part of it."

"No, Chuck." He smiled at that. "I mean it, Chuck, I'm not doing anything with anyone."

"You got no fucking choice," he said. "I already got their money. And that's something I want you to remember. The first thing you do is get the money. I've taken care of that for you this time, but in the future you'll have to be responsible for that. Now strip off your clothes."

"I'm not taking off my clothes."

I tried to sound strong but that wasn't the way I was feeling. I suddenly realized that Chuck was crazy, really insane, that he actually expected me to take off my clothes and go out there to have sex with five strangers. When he took his hand out of his trouser pocket, he was holding his pistol and pointing it at me. It was the first time anyone ever pointed a gun at me but it wouldn't be the last time.

"I'm going to shoot you right now," he said. "Unless you get out there and do what I'm telling you."

"I can't."

"Are you sure about that?" he said. "Are you really sure about that? You want to know what I think? I think you're going to take off your clothes, all of your clothes, and then you're going to go out there and fuck those five guys. And if you don't, I'm going to put a bullet into your head right now."

"Chuck, you're crazy!" I could hear a change in my voice —weakness—and I despised it. "You would never shoot me in front of five witnesses."

"Linda, don't con yourself," he said. "Those guys aren't going to say nothing to no one. They have wives and families and they're all fucking influential businessmen. You think they care what happens to some nickel-and-dime hooker who has an accident in some motel room? You think one of those guys would say he was out there waiting for a prostitute?"

"Don't do this, Chuck."

"Say your prayers," he said. "Those guys out there got

everything to lose and nothing to win by saying anything. And that about sums it up for you, too. Take off your clothes or you are one fucking dead chick!"

Suddenly I didn't doubt him. I knew he would shoot me. I was numb as I removed my clothes and put them on hangers. Then tears started to flow out of my eyes. I was trembling, really shaking, too scared even to pray. One thing I already knew about Chuck, he was not someone who'd be moved by someone else's tears. When he realized he had triumphed, his attitude went from menacing to superior and condescending. He reminded me of a little boy saying, "Ha-ha, I've got you now."

Even as I remember those moments, my heart pounds violently and I have trouble breathing. Often I've thought back to that day, and always I have this same reaction. But this day, this hour, this moment—it was the turning point of my life and I have relived it again and again.

When I look back, I always ask myself whether there had been any indications, any clues, any warnings. None. There were no hints that I was about to cross over from day to night. I remember the details with awful clarity; I remember that room as if I had never left it, as if I were still there.

And now, as always, I asked myself one question: would he *really* have shot me? Even today I think yes—yes, he would have killed me on the spot. And then I ask myself this: would I do the same thing if it were truly happening to me today? Would I go through it all again? No. No, today I would take the bullet.

I go back to that moment and I plot out escape scenarios, things that might have been done and things I might have said. I might have taken off my clothes, walked out into the room and then raced for the door. I might have picked up an ashtray and thrown it through the window and screamed for help. I might have hidden behind one of the men.

"Stop your crying before you go out there," Chuck said. "Crying is very bad for business."

Naked I walked out into the room. Two of the men waiting for me were also naked. The other three were partially undressed.

"Not bad," one of the men said. "Chuck got us a nice young one this time."

One of the naked men came over to me, put his hands under my breasts, and started to jiggle them up and down.

"Hey, lookie here," he said, "they bounce."

I had no idea what was expected of me. There was nothing in my imagination that could equal what was actually happening to me. I had a sudden vision of the barmaid at the Vegas Inn, the one with three men at the same time, and tears started to roll down my cheeks.

The man who had first greeted Chuck at the door now took him off to one side.

"What is it with this one?" he said.

"What do you mean?"

"I mean, what's going on here?" he said. "You always come up with these wild freaks and now this one doesn't even want to do it."

"Don't worry about Linda." Chuck raised his voice. "Linda will be all right."

The man who had been touching my breasts now took my elbow and led me over to the nearest bed. I opened my eyes and I saw Chuck staring at me, his face full of hatred. The man who had led me over got on top of me and entered me with no preliminaries whatsoever. The second man who was naked came over and put his thing in my mouth, just like that, no words, no explanations. He was stiff and he guided himself into and out of my mouth. By now, a third man had taken off his shorts and was coming over to the bed. He reached down, took my hand, and put it on his thing.

"Jerk me off, dear," he said.

"Don't listen to him," another voice said. "Let him jerk himself off. You just go on sucking."

"Okay," a third voice said, "let's switch now."

They were playing musical chairs with parts of my body. I had the feeling that this was no more exciting for them than it was for me; they were robots with a robot. They would busy themselves for a while at one spot, then change positions. One of the other men was still talking to Chuck, still complaining that my attitude was not all that it might have been.

The fifth man—he was about thirty-five with blond hair parted on the side—was not taking part. He stood near the other bed and most of the remarks were sent in his direction.

"Hey, what's the matter with Jim?" one of them said. "Jim can't get it up."

"Oh, I don't think Jim wants anything this crude," another voice said. "I think we're going to have to leave Jim alone with this broad."

"Yeah, old Jim's in love."

The three of them were having a fine old time goofing on Jim. Jim remained quiet and his eyes seemed sad. For a while, I almost liked him, but then he joined the party, as did the fifth man. Chuck went over to the window beside the front door and remained there, looking out, standing guard.

"Let's make a sandwich," one of the men said.

My first thought was that we were going to stop and get something to eat. By this time I had lost all appetite. But that's not what they had in mind. The man who had been calling for the sandwich lay on his back and the others put me on top of him. Then I felt another man climbing on my backside. I understood then that they were talking about a human sandwich. I had never experienced anal sex before and it really ripped me up. I began to whimper.

"Oh, lookie here," one of the men said. "We must have a new baby here."

The only one who seemed to realize that I wasn't doing this by choice, that this was just something happening to me, was the man who had been talking to Chuck. But it didn't matter to him. He was the top half of the sandwich.

The three animals who had come on first cared about nothing but getting their jollies. I can no longer remember their faces. They never talked to me directly. They talked to each other over and around me, as though I was a piece of meat.

Most of the time my eyes were tightly closed. They didn't mind. They were so into getting their rocks off that they wouldn't have cared if I was an inflatable plastic doll, a puppet. They picked me up and moved me here and there; they spread my legs this way and that; they shoved their things at me and into me.

Three of the animals were constant and persistent, always coming at me, not even resting between times. The other two would back off from time to time. Two of the men got their biggest thrill by working themselves up to the point of coming and then shooting their sperm all over my body and rubbing it in.

I had never been so frightened in my life. Every time I looked over at Chuck, his look scared me all over again. I was scared by what was happening to me at that moment and what might happen to me next. Even though it was all too clearly happening to me, I couldn't understand *why* it was happening. I couldn't believe that five human beings would do this to another human being.

"Hey, let's try to get in two at once," one said.

"Nah, that's impossible," another said.

"Crowded, but not impossible."

And that's what they tried next. I had no idea what they were talking about. But two of the men tried to pry their way ino me at the same time. I can't tell you whether they succeeded.

That's when I went numb. A lot was still happening to my body but it stopped meaning anything to me. My breasts were being mauled and I stopped feeling that. It was as if my body belonged to someone else. A voice from a great distance was saying, "Stick this in your mouth, darling," but that no longer concerned me—it seemed as though it was someone else's mouth opening, someone else sucking, someone else swallowing.

Finally they began to tire and to take occasional breaks.

Maybe they were getting bored. After all, I had only so many hands and only so many openings and before too long, all possibilities were exhausted. Then Chuck came over to the bed and looked down at me.

"You're a fucking mess," he said. "Go take a shower."

I picked myself up from the bed and went to the bathroom. I had never wanted a shower so much, and I had never scrubbed myself so hard. I scrubbed at my skin where they had come all over me. Then I scrubbed at the rest of me. I wished I could melt into the shower drain and disappear. At that moment I wouldn't have minded dying.

I was filled with hurt. And I kept turning to God. As far as I was concerned, it was His fault. He had put me here.

All the time I was in the shower, I was talking to God. "Why, God, why? Please tell me why." I had asked God to help me and He hadn't helped at all. Well, maybe I shouldn't say that. He did help me get through it. He did help me survive. So I guess He was helping me out after all. But it took me a long time to come to that belief.

When I went into the room to dress, the men were gone and Chuck was counting out the money on the bed. Each of the men had been charged $40.00, but Chuck had only $180. The one who had been complaining about my attitude had demanded a refund and Chuck had given him back half his money.

I was still speechless and in shock. I had no idea that human beings did such things. I knew that a prostitute offered sex for money, but somehow I figured they would make *love*—that there would be kissing and caressing and some gentleness.

I didn't say a word to Chuck. I followed him out of the room and to the car. The minute we were in the car, with the doors closed, he turned to me and started yelling.

"Sit up! Sit up straight when I'm talking to you!"

I didn't say anything.

"Don't you know how to do anything right?" he went on. "You were lying there like some vegetable, like some fucking turnip. You're no good and you never will be. You don't know what to do and you don't know how to do it. What the fuck is it with you anyway? You better start getting your shit together, Linda."

I didn't say a word, couldn't say a word, had forgotten all words. I could still feel those hands all over me, pressing me, squeezing me, milking me.

"Sit straight when I'm talking to you! Any common hooker off the street somewhere would've done better. You know the difference between you and a pro? A pro would've taken control. She would've been coming up with the weird ideas, the positions. The way you were, they hadda do all the fucking work."

No words. I went over exactly what had happened. The man I was living with had pulled a gun on me, had forced me to undress, had thrown me into a room with five strange males, had watched them rape me over and over, and now he was angry because I hadn't been exciting enough for them. *Good God!*

"Those guys'll never come back to me again," Chuck was saying. "Not after today. We can write them off. You know what I was trying to do today? I was trying to get a business started. *Our* business. That's all. Just trying to get a business started. You know how you fucking get a business started? You show five guys a good time, that's what you do. Then each of them goes out and tells two more people. Then you got ten, fifteen, guys. And they talk it up and then you got a little business going there. You know what these guys are going to tell their friends after today? Nothing, that's what. You're ruining my fucking business."

Still I said nothing.

"You're supposed to be freaky!" he said. "You're supposed to enjoy it. You're not supposed to be laying there like some kind of dead log. Shape up, cunt, I'm warning you. Next time better be different. Next time better be better."

*Next* time? Oh, God, what next time?

# *five*

---

I didn't have to wait long for the next time. The following day, Chuck introduced me to a visitor, an old friend who managed a truck-rental business, and my name became Tracy at this point.

"This is Harry," Chuck said. "I told Harry that you'd make him happy, that you'd do anything he wants to do. So I'm going to split for a while and leave you two kids alone."

Chuck walked out of the living room and an instant later I heard the front door slam. I was alone with my first paying customer, my first trick. Harry thumbed through his wallet and fished out two twenty-dollar bills.

"Chuck said it was forty," Harry said. "Is forty all right with you."

"I guess so."

"Your name is Tracy, right?" I nodded. "Yeah, well, I was sure glad to hear that Chuck was back in the business. Just like old times."

If I was seeing Harry under any other circumstances, he would've seemed nice enough. He was soft-spoken and that has always been an important quality with me. But at this moment he was not even on my mind that much; I was hardly thinking about him. I could think of only one thing—

Chuck had finally left me alone. Well, not *entirely* alone. There was one matter to take care of first.

I took off my jeans and blouse and laid them over a chair. Was I supposed to take off the rest or was he? I had no idea. I went over to the bed and sat down on the edge of it and waited for him to come over and do whatever he was going to do to me.

"Tracy, would you mind a little friendly advice," Harry said to me. "Chuck tells me you're just starting out so you probably don't know what you're supposed to do yet. But the thing is, you should at least be friendly. In fact, you should fake like you really want it."

"Please don't talk," I said. "Just do what you want to."

"Suit yourself."

The way he said that, I knew that my attitude wasn't right and that would undoubtedly get back to Chuck. I was scared and I was dry but Harry went right into me. It hurt at first and it didn't get better. The expression on his face told me that he wasn't enjoying it much more than I was. But he went on anyway, pumping away. I lay there lifeless, letting him do all the work. Before too much longer, I would learn to fake it, even to be aggressive, just like the other hookers, but right then I just wanted him to finish and get off me. The moment he was done, I rolled out from under him and went to get my clothes.

"What's this, a race?"

He seemed to find everything I did very funny. But finally he stopped laughing, got up, got himself dressed and got himself out the front door. I counted to ten, then followed him. As I opened the door, I heard a small noise behind me. A hand on my shoulder. Chuck hadn't left. He had been standing there in the hallway the whole time.

"Going out?" he said. "Going out for a little walk?"

"*Chuck!*" That was a small scream. "I was just going out to look for you."

"Well, cunt, you found me."

He grabbed my arm and yanked me back into the living

room. Then he started punching my body over and over again until I collapsed on the floor. It was hurting so much that I couldn't cry. That's when he went into the kitchen to get a butcher knife.

"You know something, cunt? I've decided not to waste a bullet on you. I've decided to cut up your fucking face instead. If you get out of line just one more time—one more time—I'm going to fuck up your face so bad that no one'll ever look at you again."

"Don't do that, Chuck."

"Oh, tell me why the fuck not," he said, mocking me. "You're useless. You're no fucking good. *No fucking good!* You can't even fuck good. You're so ugly that all my customers will want their money back. You got scars all over your belly, your tits are pancakes, you're no fucking good at all. I'd be doing the world a favor, just putting you out of your fucking misery."

"Please, please, Chuck."

From this point on, not a day went by that I didn't hear more of that. Every day I either got raped, beaten, kicked, punched, smacked, choked, degraded, or yelled at. Sometimes, I got all of the above. Strangely enough, what bothered me most was the endless verbal abuse. He never let up: I was *so* dumb; I was *so* ugly; I was *so* fat; I was *so* thin; I was *so* flat-chested, and I was *so* lucky to have him taking care of me. The constant yelling took everything out of me.

To buy a share of my nightmare the tricks paid from $25.00 to $150.00—depending. Depending on what the customer requested, depending on whether he was a regular or not, depending on Chuck's mood. I had as much to do with the money as a teller at a bank; I got it from one man and passed it along to another man. That was the end of my contact with any money. These financial transactions would occur three times on an average day.

Before long, as his business grew, Chuck was able to add to his staff. The first arrival was a young girl named Moonshine. Moonshine was strictly a volunteer. She had been making love with a married man who had been paying her rent. A second boyfriend started taking care of her telephone bill. There was someone else to pay the electric bill and a fourth man who gave her a rented car to use. Before long, Moonshine had many steady visitors and no bills to pay. She came to Chuck with the idea of expanding her horizons and perhaps even getting some take-home pay. There was nothing Moonshine wouldn't do to further her career.

At any rate, Moonshine was there to share the work load. Then came Debbie. And Melody. Now you might think that this would take some of the pressure off me. But there was more to it than that. You see, Chuck had his own system of distributing the tricks. If a customer was handsome or clean-cut or just young, Chuck would send him off with one of the other working girls. But if he was an eighty-year-old man on crutches, or a 350-pound mama's boy, or a customer asking whether we supplied whips, then he'd turn to me: "This one's for you, Linda."

There are so many things about Chuck Traynor that I'll never understand. He would fix me up with creeps and degenerates; he would watch them rape me through a hole in the mirror; but he would bristle with jealousy if a young or good-looking man paid any attention to me.

"You know something," I told him once. "You're jealous."

"Bullshit!"

"No, I mean it. You *are* jealous. If I didn't know better, I'd swear you had some normal human feelings."

"Better not count on that, cunt."

I didn't. And, in truth, I began to forget what normal people with normal feelings were like. One trick came in every week and asked for his "eleven-year-old friend." And every week he would hand me a script that he had written and I would have to say the lines to him.

Lines like: "Please don't hurt me, sir, I'm only eleven years old." Lines like: "Oooh, you're so big and strong—please, sir, don't take away my cherry." Lines like—well, you get the idea.

And then there was Greg. Greg was thirty-eight years old, a successful architect, and he hired two of us. Greg had a slightly different script. One of the girls—usually Melody—waited outside in the living room while I went into the bed with Greg. Melody would then come to the door and I would have to say, "Ooooh, golly, Greg—your mommy's here." And Melody would come storming over to the bed and strip the sheet away from us and say, "Gregory! What are you doing with this cheap girl? I think I'm going to have to spank you!" The following week Melody and I might switch roles with my playing the mother and her playing the cheap girl.

I guess this is where I got my early dramatic training. However, I didn't always understand the other characters' motivations. One of the least demanding customers owned a huge resort hotel and paid $150.00 a week. Every week Chuck would take me to a penthouse suite in the man's hotel and wait for me outside the door. All I had to do was take off my clothes and take a bubble bath in one of those circular sunken tubs. The trick sat and watched me soap myself for a full hour and that was the extent of our involvement.

There was another customer who shared Chuck's sickness; he got off on pain. He paid $75.00 for the pleasure of making anal love to me while hitting me. I had no idea how I was supposed to react to this sort of thing. I didn't yet know I was supposed to scream in pain one minute and scream with joy the next; beg for mercy and beg for more at the same time. Before he left, the trick complained to Chuck about my amateurishness.

"Lemme make it right for you," Chuck said. "Come back tomorrow and you can have her for nothing."

"Thanks, but no thanks," the trick said. "When you get someone new in, give me a call."

Customer complaints led to more severe beatings than usual. Also to a brand new line of verbal abuse: "You useless cunt, I can't even give you away for free!"

My inexperience did cost us several customers, a fact that didn't disturb me in the least. Much of the time I couldn't begin to imagine what possible pleasure they would get out of the strange things they wanted me to do. One trick who lived alone on a houseboat asked me to sit on his face and urinate in his mouth. I couldn't do that. I tried but just couldn't do it. The trick got angrier and angrier, and, finally, he screamed at me to go into the bathroom and put it in a glass. I returned with a glassful of urine and he drank it down. Then he told me to get off his boat and never come back. I was happy to oblige.

Since Chuck would never beat me up when we were away from his house, I was always pleased when the trick wanted to meet his "date" at a motel or an apartment. Just knowing that Chuck wasn't staring at me through his little peephole helped some. And there was always the possibility of escape, the thought that he might slip up and leave me unguarded for a few minutes. Still and all, the trips from home were never what you might call pleasure trips. For one thing, I never knew what might be waiting for me on the other side of a door.

Early in August, Chuck drove me to a private home in South Miami. The door was answered by a fat man with oiled black hair, maybe fifty-five years old. The fat man—his name was Leonard Campagno, also known as Lenny Camp—lived in incredible squalor. His living room was filled with boxes and crates. Newspapers were a carpet over the floor and cats were everywhere. Dishes with food still on them were spread over the table and piled in the sink. I could see cat hairs in the sugar bowl.

Lenny led us through this litter to a bedroom in the back. It was not quite as sleazy as the rest of the house. At least there were clean sheets on the bed. Floodlights had been set up around the bed and were pointing down at it.

"Get her undressed now," Lenny said to Chuck. "Tell her to take off all her things."

People seemed to be doing that more and more often, speaking around me as if I weren't in the room. Sometimes I felt almost invisible.

"Okay, Useless," Chuck said. "Get undressed. We're going to do some pictures here."

"What kind of pictures?"

"Picture-pictures," he said. "You'll see."

"Chuck, what kind of pictures?"

"The kind of pictures where you got to take your clothes off first, okay? Now move it."

"You told me never to let anyone take my picture."

"Yeah, that's anyone *else*."

At least a dozen times Chuck had told me there were two things I should never do. I should never let anyone take my picture, and I should never sign my name to anything. He said those were two things that would always come back and haunt you later on.

"This here is different," he explained. "Take your clothes off and go into the bathroom and try to put your face on straight."

And that was that. There never was a way to argue with Chuck, no way to even discuss anything. I had no notion of what was going to happen here, only that I was going to take my clothes off and be photographed. In all our time together, Chuck never bothered to explain anything. Mine was no longer one of those lives where you could tell what was going to happen next.

I was in the bathroom, naked, putting on some lipstick, when the door opened behind me. My visitor was a tiny girl, five feet tall and very slim, brown-haired, about eighteen years old and also naked.

"Hi," she said. "I'm Chicklet."

"I'm Linda."

Chicklet was full of energy, a non-stop talker. All the time she put on her makeup, she was telling her life story. She considered herself a "model." She said the day before, while she was being photographed, she had ripped off a bracelet from the photographer and he had never even noticed. She said the day before that she had a "session" with six guys at the same time.

Finally she seemed to notice that I wasn't returning any of the conversation. She glanced at me in the mirror and stopped putting on her lipstick.

"Hey, what's the matter, honey?"

"I don't even know what they're going to do to me out there."

"Take your picture is all," Chicklet said. "Me and you are having our pictures taken."

I was no longer as naive as I had been a few months earlier. I knew we were not talking about high school yearbook pictures, and I knew that I wasn't there to play patty-cake. I had already figured out that I was going to be photographed in compromising positions—but *which* compromising positions? So many strangers had been using my body in so many different ways that I didn't think anything would ever shock me again. Wrong.

"You've done this before, right?" Chicklet asked.

"Done what before?"

"You've been with another chick before, right?" Chicklet could see that she was drawing a blank. "You've balled another chick, am I right?"

I burst into tears. That was my only answer. Chicklet came over to me and put her arm around my shoulder. Suddenly her voice was very soothing.

"Hey, hey, there's nothing to worry about," she said. "These are all *stills*. We don't have to *do* anything. We don't have to be moving at all. Lenny tells us what he wants and we just go through the motions. You don't have to be into it at all. All you've got to do is relax. So relax, willya? It's not going to be so terrible. You don't think I'm like ugly, do you?"

"No," I said.

"Well, stop it with the crying," Chicklet said. "We'll just let things go down the way they're gonna and if you don't dig something, we'll like fake it. I'll start the old ball rolling and you just do whatever, just like me."

I followed Chicklet out into the bedroom. The fat man,

two different cameras roped around his neck, was waiting for us. Chuck was leaning against a wall, staring right through me. I think his whole pleasure in life was watching me react to things. The floodlights were on, an explosion of light over the double bed.

"Okay, girls," Lenny said. "Why don't we start off with a few little kisserinos?"

We did as we were told. Just a few little kisserinos. As that was happening, I made myself go numb. I thought of myself as a metal robot, no human feelings at all, and that worked for a while. I was feeling nothing. A skinny naked girl was kissing me on the mouth and I felt nothing at all. She tried to put her tongue in my mouth but she learned that you can't pry open a robot's lips.

"Okay, Linda," Lenny said. *Click, click, click.* "Put your right hand over there on Chicklet's breast. No, no, *no!* Wouldja at least try to make it look natural?"

*Natural?* Try to make it look natural? How could it look natural, my putting my hand on another woman's breast? What on earth would make that natural? I couldn't imagine what to do.

"C'm'on, Linda, get into it," Lenny said. *Click, click, click.* "Chuck, couldja tell your cunt there to get into this. She could at least look like she's getting her rocks off."

"*Linda!*" That was a warning.

"Chicklet, what's with you two?" Lenny asked.

"Hey, lemme talk to Linda for a minute, she's just shy." The lights were turned off then and Chicklet walked with me over to the side of the room. "Look, Linda, lemme give you some advice. The best way—the easiest way—to get through something like this is to like get into it, really get into it, and then it'll be over and done with. Otherwise, we're gonna be hanging around here all day and we still have to do the sixty-nine shots."

The sixty-nine shots? I wasn't ready for something like that. I could be a robot through the kissing and even through touching her breast. I could go through the motions and erase them from my mind almost as they were happening. But when it came to something like sixty-nine, something that personal with another woman, it really blew my mind. I had never even let a man do that to me.

"I can't do that."

"Listen to me." Chicklet lowered her voice as though we were conspirators. *"Just do it!* We'll just go through the motions together—you're gonna have to anyway—and then it'll be over with and you can forget all about it. Look, when you go down on me, just fake it. You know, you don't have to actually do nothing. I won't tell anyone."

I'm not sure whether Chicklet was conning me or just calming me down, but we both knew there was no choice. I'm not sure why this bothered me more than the things I was doing as a hooker. All I know is that it was far worse. I couldn't imagine being with another woman. At the same time I was wondering what they were doing with the pictures they were taking. Where would they go? Would my mother and father ever see them? I had an awful feeling that the pictures would someday be used against me. Whether they were or not, they made this part of my life real, part of some record, uneraseable.

*Click, click, click.*

This was a day of many firsts. The first photographs. The first sex with another woman. And there was still another first to come. When the fat photographer had enough pictures of the two of us together, he went into another room and came back with something that he started to strap onto Chicklet. It was a strap-on, make-believe, male sex organ. My first dildo. The dildo jutted out like a telephone pole when it was fastened to Chicklet's small frame. Then, assuming the male role, something she did with no difficulty at all, Chicklet got on top of me and put the dildo inside of me. The fat man came in very close with his camera. *Click, click, click.*

So there I was, being photographed by a fat degenerate

while a skinny little girl with a make-believe penis was having sex with me, and I looked over at Chuck. He was watching the scene with a very superior expression. At moments like these, the lowest spots in my life, whenever I saw Chuck watching me, I would become aware of just one thing, his missing finger. Under normal circumstances—say we were just driving along in his car—I would never notice it. But whenever Chuck got me into a bad spot, that missing finger loomed large, casting a shadow over my mind. Now all I could see was the deformed hand, the absent finger.

Chicklet was my first female sex partner. Not my last. As soon as Chuck saw how much pain this experience caused me, he made sure that it became a key part of my repertoire. Many men like to rent that particular fantasy—two women making love to each other while the man becomes excited and then joins in. A few weeks earlier I didn't know what "bisexual" meant and suddenly I was having sex with a half dozen women and several dozen men.

I only liked one of the women I was coupled with—and the sex itself had nothing whatever to do with my liking her.

Melody was the first person to help me in any way. One day she saw Chuck hit me and that was enough for her. From that moment on, she was my friend. Melody was a strange kind of a girl to be a hooker. She was very intelligent and always carried a book to read with her, even on jobs.

Melody was cute rather than sexy looking—about five-two, light brown curly hair, pug nose, non-stop smile. She reminded me of a high school cheerleader. But the main thing about her was that she was smart, way too smart to ever become one of Chuck's girls. Melody was a madame with a small operation of her own; she lived in and worked out of a tastefully decorated four-room apartment. When her customers were too weird for her, Melody transferred them over to Chuck's operation. If they were really weird, disgustingly so, Chuck made sure that they eventually found their way to me.

From the beginning, Melody seemed to take a personal interest in me. Whenever she had a job that required more than one hooker, she would call up Chuck and put in a request for me. Chuck would drive me to the meeting and wait nearby. He was never far away, but at least I was out of his sight for a time.

Melody seemed to understand Chuck very well. She knew just what to tell him to get me off on a job with her. She would tell Chuck the most degenerate stuff she could think up and he would leap at the bait. For example, she would tell him that she had a customer who wanted to tie up two girls and urinate on them, and Chuck would say, "Far *out!* Why don't you take Linda on that one?" Or she would say, "This John is too much—he wants to give some girl an enema." And Chuck would say, "Yeah? Well, Linda would like to do that trick."

There was one trick we shared every week. This was an old guy in a wheelchair, barely able to stand up. He would hire six or seven girls and each girl would get a fifty-dollar bill. One girl would stand behind him, holding him upright, while all the other girls except me would be on the carpet, kissing each other and making love. My job was to kneel in front of him and suck him off. Melody would give me that task because she knew that I found that easier than being with another woman.

And sometimes, when we finished a job like that, there'd be a few minutes to talk to Melody without Chuck listening.

"This is all really awful for you," she said one day. "Isn't there any way you can get away from Chuck?"

"You know Chuck."

"I know a dozen Chucks," she said, "a hundred Chucks, and they're all monsters."

Whenever I started talking about my life, I found myself fighting to hold back the tears. But it was no use; there was no holding them back. And then I couldn't hold back the words. I told Melody everything that had happened: how he kept me prisoner; how he watched me through a peephole; how he beat me constantly; how he threatened to kill me, and how he swore to murder my parents if I ever managed to get away.

"And it's getting worse," I said. "He keeps thinking up worse things for me to do. And now he wants *me* to think up weird things—he says if I don't think up at least one new 'freaky' thing every day, he'll beat me."

"He's a real sicko," Melody said. "Sometimes I get the feeling that the world is full of sicko people."

"There can't be anyone else as bad as Chuck."

"Don't kid yourself," she said. "Look, I'll tell you the kind of thing you tell Chuck. Tell him that today I tied all the other girls together, locking them into strange positions, and then the old guy began beating on everyone with a cane. Tell him that some of the girls were really screaming; one was yelling, 'No, no more, no more pain!' And another one was saying, 'Hit me! Hit me! Harder, harder!' Tell him that some of the girls got very excited and had orgasms."

It was a strange way for a friendship to start. Melody told me every unnatural act she had ever heard of, and then she made up some brand new ones just for Chuck. And almost every day she managed to find me a trick in a hotel or an apartment, a job that got me away from Chuck, if only for a little while.

Sometimes, the way things worked out, I'd rather have stayed with Chuck. Melody turned over one of her $150-a-week customers to me, a guy who weighed nearly 400 pounds. Chuck was happy to have me do that one for two reasons: it was so much money, and it was so revolting.

To make up for jobs like that one, Melody would also take me along on her easiest tricks. There was Leo, a retired clothing manufacturer who had a condominium on the beach. When you first arrived, Leo made you go through closets filled with dresses, gowns, and lingerie. You were allowed to select whatever you liked. Then you modeled that for

Leo, marching up and down in front of him, turning this way and that, until he said, "All right, girlie, take off all your clothes."

When Melody and I had removed our clothing, we would pretend to make love while Leo got turned on. Afterwards, he would give us each thirty dollars and the clothes we had modeled; that clothing was the only payment I was ever allowed to keep.

I knew that someday God would get me away from Chuck but until then, until God made His move, my only help came from Melody. She kept thinking up new perversions for me to tell Chuck. She was like that girl in *The Arabian Nights*, the one who had to tell the king a brand new story every day, only the stories Melody told me were not exactly fairy tales.

"Linda," she said, "you know what a dildo is?"

"Yes."

"Well, they have these dildoes with two heads on them."

"Two heads?"

"Yes, try to follow this, Linda. The two-headed dildoes are about this long and this big around. Tell him that the trick had one of those with him and you had to insert both ends of it at once . . ."

Okay, so it wasn't exactly *The Arabian Nights*. In fact, some of the perversions were so elaborate that I couldn't believe my ears. I was sure that Chuck would start laughing at me when I told him a story like that. But that wasn't what happened at all. His eyes would go glassy and then he'd get sexually excited.

Every time Melody and I turned a trick together, we would find time for a little talk. Melody had a book—*The Female Eunuch* by Germaine Greer—that she wanted me to read. The first time Chuck saw me looking at it, he tore it from my hands and threw it away.

There were other times with Melody when I felt very uncomfortable. One day after our regular session with Leo, she reached out and touched my hand.

"You know something?" she said. "I really liked that today. I couldn't help myself. It's just that when I'm with you, I really start to get it on."

"Don't tell me about that, please, Melody."

"I can't help it, I'm starting to really love you. I *do* love you. You're so beautiful and nice. I've been with a lot of girls but when I'm with you, I get a very warm feeling. Do you know what I mean?"

"Please don't tell me about it, Melody. You're my only friend, and I don't want anything to happen to that friendship. I need you as a friend."

"But I could do so much for you, Linda. You're going to get away from Chuck someday. As sure as I'm sitting here, you're going to be free of him. And then you're going to need a place to stay. You could stay with me and I'd take care of you. You would learn to love me."

"I can't. I couldn't. Please don't."

"Linda, honey, I know how you feel, believe me. I know you're not into being with another woman, not now, but there's always a chance that you'll change your mind."

"I won't change my mind."

"If you do, you'll know where to find me."

There were a few encounters like this one, and they're the reason that I don't look back at Melody as a close friend— but at least she was a human being with me. She cared and that was enough. Maybe she was doing things for her own benefit. But whatever her motives were, she did manage to get Chuck Traynor off my back and out of my sight from time to time. Escape seemed a possibility.

And escape was all I was thinking about those days. Some of the people who know my story wonder about my inability to get away; they wonder whether I didn't begin to enjoy my new life. They wonder whether it is possible to go through weeks and months of incredible sexual activity and receive no sensual pleasure at all.

Did I enjoy any of it? Did I ever have a moment's pleasure? I want to state this as clearly as I can. There was no pleasure.

There was no love, no affection, no normal sex with anyone from the day I met Chuck Traynor until the day I finally got away. I did not have a single orgasm for six or seven years. I never had any enjoyment from any of it at all.

In fact, the only trick I could ever have a decent conversation with was a mortician named Jason. The first time Jason came to the house he told he just wanted to talk to me, nothing more. He didn't touch me that first day, but he still gave me a ten-dollar tip.

"My problem is that I'm an incurable romantic," Jason told me. "I couldn't stand the thought of going to bed with a prostitute, so I'm going to ask you for a favor. Whenever I come to see you, I want you to pretend that we're lovers, that we've just fallen madly in love."

"I've done stranger things."

"Okay," he said, "and next time around, we won't just talk. But for today I just wanted to get to know you."

And so Jason and I had what he called "our love affair." He was extremely romantic, always calling me "lover" and "darling." He was extremely upset when he learned that Chuck was spying on us and insisted that we meet at a motel. That was just fine with me.

Even though he was a paying customer, Jason never did a cruel thing to me. At first, the fact that he was a mortician gave me the willies but that feeling faded as I spent more and more time with him. Pleasure? No, it was never a pleasure— but it was a relief. He was a gentleman and he wasn't into anything too weird, unless bringing me flowers and calling me "sweetheart" could be considered weird.

One day, as his hour of romance was coming to an end, Jason made the mistake of asking me a question I had already heard a dozen times.

"How'd a nice girl like you ever get involved in doing this?"

"You wouldn't want to know."

"Try me."

"Okay," I said. "In the first place, you should know I'm

not here because I want to be. I'm here because I'm a prisoner of Chuck Traynor who just happens to be insane."

I stopped there, allowed that to settle in, and watched for his reaction. He wasn't pleased. I could tell that this was not the kind of thing he was paying to hear.

"Go on," he said.

As the story poured out of me, his mood went from serious to sad to deeply concerned.

"Maybe I could help you," he said.

"How could you help me?"

"I have a little cabin up in the woods," he said. "You could go up there and hide out for a while."

"Where in the woods? What woods?"

"It's in southern Georgia," he said. "Only about seven hours away. There's just one thing. I wouldn't want Chuck to know that I was connected with this at all. I'll tell you the truth, he scares me. But you could stay up there in the cabin and later I'd join you."

"I know how this might work." My mind was going a mile a minute now. "You could arrange to meet me in a motel with a back way out. You'd just stay in your room, and I'd skip out the back. When Chuck came looking for me, you'd just tell him I never showed up. If you were still there in the room, he wouldn't think that you were involved."

"Yes, you could live in my cabin then," Jason was saying. "And then when I joined you, we could become *real* lovers. We could be together all the time and really be in love."

The way he was going on, my mind started to play tricks on me: Perhaps I was getting into something far worse? What kind of man pays $45.00 to rent a woman anyhow? What kind of man prefers make-believe love over real love? Then I thought about his being a mortician—maybe he was one of those guys who liked dead bodies; Chuck had told me about them. Maybe he was just another super-freak who wanted to get me up in the woods of Georgia so that he could kill me.

The bottom line: I chickened out.

"Jason, let's think about this a little while," I said.

When I *do* think about it now, when I go back to moments like that, I start to jam—my head gets all jammed up. Why didn't I take my chances with Jason? Or with Melody? How could it possibly have been any worse than what happened to me? Was I so terrified that everything in life scared me?

Life with Chuck never improved. I learned to settle for the smallest imaginable triumphs, the absence of pain or the momentary lessening of terror.

In time, I learned to satisfy men like Chuck—men who got their kicks from pain. I learned how to do this without suffering too much pain myself. Chuck had taught me how to relax my throat muscles so that I wouldn't gag during oral sex. I set about teaching all of my muscles to relax. It got so that I could relax any set of muscles at will.

So when Chuck started putting his fist inside of me, I was able to relax and cut back on the pain. And when he finally found a two-headed dildo of his very own—I was surprised to learn that it actually existed—I learned how to relax so that even that wouldn't hurt too much.

But I wouldn't tell Chuck that. On the contrary, I would scream for mercy, and he would become hard and ejaculate almost instantly; then he would leave me alone for a while. I was becoming quite a little actress. I learned that it was never enough to fake pain, you had to fake pleasure at the same time: "Oh, Chuck, that hurts . . . that hurts too much . . . but please don't stop." That kind of nonsense.

In a strange way, even the sword-swallowing, deep-throat techniques that Chuck had taught me could work to my advantage. There were times when Chuck would make me work parties with maybe fifteen men and two chicks. This is still difficult for me to talk about, and I apologize in advance for it, but I don't know a more polite way to put it: I found it easier to suck a man's cock than to let him put his thing inside of me. I was a virgin until I was almost twenty years old, and only a couple of men before Chuck had ever made love to me. What I found most degrading was when a man put his thing inside of me and came. The thought of fifteen men doing that in one night was more than I could tolerate. I had a choice of which was better for me to do, which made me feel more comfortable. And sucking cock made me feel more comfortable than being fucked.

Because of my ability to totally relax my throat muscles, I became very popular with men who were into oral sex. Over and over again I heard tricks say, "Nobody's ever done that to me before." And of course they would want to call a friend so that he could have it done to him, too.

Chuck was very pleased with this. He called it word-of-mouth advertising.

# *six*

---

Often I'm asked why I didn't escape. Behind that question there's an attitude, a presumption. I can see it in the face asking the question. The questioner always has the sure knowledge that this could never have happened to him or to her. They would have been strong enough and smart enough and resourceful enough to have gotten away. In fact, if the truth be known, they would never have allowed themselves to get into this kind of predicament in the first place. Once, during a grand jury hearing in California, I was asked the question point-blank: "How come you never got away?"

And I answered point-blank: "Because it's kind of hard to get away when there's a gun pointed at your head."

There was always a gun pointed at my head. Even when no gun could be seen, there was a gun pointed at my head. I can understand why some people have such trouble accepting this as the truth. When I was younger, when I heard about a woman being raped, my secret feeling was that that could never happen to me. I would never *permit* it to happen. Now I realize that can be about as meaningful as saying I won't allow an earthquake or I won't permit an avalanche.

It's impossible for people to understand real terror unless

they've felt it, lived it, tasted it. It's impossible to picture your own death until that possibility is real, until the car is careening or the plane is falling or you are looking at a madman holding a loaded gun. Today, when I'm sitting home quietly with my husband and child, it's again difficult to conceive of anyone forcing me into unspeakable perversions. But I know that it did happen once, and I know something else: It could happen again—to me or to you.

At first I was certain that God would help me escape but in time my faith was shaken. I became more and more frightened, scared of everything. The very thought of trying to escape was terrifying. I had been degraded every possible way, stripped of all dignity, reduced to an animal and then to a vegetable. Whatever strength I had began to disappear. Simple survival took everything; making it all the way to tomorrow was a victory.

The experience has enabled me to understand many events that others seem to find incomprehensible. I have no difficulty relating to what happened to Patty Hearst; I have the feeling that we could be the closet of friends. Recently when several Playboy bunnies in Great Gorge, New Jersey, were drugged, photographed and forced to work as whores, I could understand the process. I can even comprehend the Jonestown massacre, hundreds of people standing in line, waiting to drink their cyanide. I know what inhuman doses of fear and pain can do to any human being.

Still, there were several times when I did try to escape. My first opportunity came after I had been working as a hooker for almost a month.

The newest addition to Chuck's stable was a twenty-year-old, a veteran hooker named Kitty. Kitty—blonde, thin, intense and streetwise—had worked for Chuck earlier and was now returning after a year out on the streets, returning and bringing her own string of steady customers with her.

Kitty was tough and independent. When she realized that I was working against my will, she seemed sympathetic.

"I think that's terrible," she said. "I don't think anyone should *have* to do anything."

One of Kitty's private customers was a seventy-five-year-old retired druggist named Albert who lived with his sister in an apartment not far from the beach. Whenever his sister went away for a visit, Albert would get on the phone to Kitty. This time he asked Kitty whether she could bring "a second girl" and Chuck decided this would be an assignment for me.

Whenever I went to a new apartment building or hotel, I mentally charted the possible escape routes. This was a two-story, U-shaped building with only a single entranceway. You walked through a set of arches, then about fifteen feet into a lobby, then up one flight of stairs to the apartment. As Chuck parked the car in front of the building, I realized that I would be out of his range of vision for several moments both coming and going.

Sudden panic. I needed time, time to figure out a plan, but there was no time. There was only now. Kitty and I walked from the car toward the arches framing the entrance. I didn't want anything to come as a surprise to Kitty.

"Kitty, you know I don't want to do any of this. There's only one reason I'm doing it at all—if I weren't doing this, I'd be dead. Chuck says he'll kill me if I ever try to get away but I've got to try anyway. If this keeps up, I'm going to be dead anyway."

"What can I do?"

"Nothing," I said. "It's just that I wanted to warn you. I'm going to try and get away here, and I don't want you to be too surprised by anything that happens."

"Oh, Chuck's really going to be pissed," she said.

By this time we were up at the top of the stairs and Albert was waving us into his apartment. He was a short man, thin with a protruding pot belly. His bald head was rimmed with black hair. Albert was wearing an undershirt and a pair of shapeless old-man trousers. His apartment reminded me of the set of an old movie. The lamps were covered with heavy fabric shades, and the overstuffed sofa had white doilies on the arm rests. The stink of cologne was everywhere: on Albert, on the furniture and in the air.

As we walked through the living room toward the bedroom, my eyes were darting everywhere looking for an exit. We followed Albert into his bedroom and he turned his back on us and lifted his undershirt over his head.

"The money's on the bureau," he said. "You girls just help yourself."

"Just a minute," I said. "Just a minute, Albert, I've got to speak to you."

"No, you don't," Kitty tried to interrupt me. "Not now. We don't have to say anything at all, not yet. We just have to make nice to my sweetie here."

"No . . ."

"What's the trouble, bubala?" Albert asked.

"I'm not a hooker." I realized how absurd that sounded even as I said it. "There's a guy out there in the car who has been forcing me to do these things. You've got to help me escape."

"What're you saying?" He turned to Kitty. "What's this young girl saying?"

"Don't mind her," Kitty said. "She's just kidding."

"I'm not kidding," I said.

"She's not kidding," Albert informed Kitty.

"This is the truth," I went on. "I'm a prisoner and I'm pleading with you to help me. There's a man sitting out there right now, waiting for me, and he's a killer. Is there a back way out of here?"

"Better you should use the front door," Albert said. "Better you should use the front door right now."

Kitty was glancing at the envelope of money left on top of the bureau. Should she or shouldn't she? She knew as well as I did what Chuck would do if we came down without the money.

"I'm going to use your telephone," I said. "I'm going to call the police."

Albert moved pretty well for a senior citizen. I managed to dial 0 for Operator and then his hand came crushing down on the receiver.

"No, no, no!" His voice was shrill. "No coppers, absolutely no coppers here. Look, miss, you don't know my sister. She don't want no coppers, and no crazy people, in her house. You girls go and get out of here now and just leave bygones be bygones."

As the two of us came up to the arches, I began to flip out. I have never been so scared. Then I saw that Chuck had moved his car and was parked about a hundred yards away from the entranceway. He seemed to be dozing behind the wheel. There was a chance and I took it. I felt that I had nothing to lose, there would be a beating no matter what.

"*Chuck!* Chuck, hurry up!" I could hear Kitty screaming. "Chuck, she's trying to get away. *Hurry!*"

I might have made it. If Kitty had remained quiet just one minute more—even a half-minute more—I would have had a shot. But before I reached the corner, Chuck Traynor caught up with me and his grip burnt itself into my upper arm.

Once we were back in the car, Chuck asked me no questions. He didn't have to. What I had done was self-explanatory. Besides, Kitty was only too anxious to fill in the details. She told Chuck what I had said on the way into the building, what I had told the old man, even how I had tried to call the police.

At first I gave Kitty the benefit of the doubt. I thought that it must be panic that made her talk, fear of Chuck's anger. But that wasn't the reason. She took too much relish in telling the full story. She was just making brownie points. She wanted to be *numero uno* with Chuck.

Later, when Melody heard this story, Kitty got a comeuppance of sorts. She was blacklisted by all the other hookers in the Miami area. It doesn't seem like such a terrible punishment at this moment, but Kitty was drummed right out of the business.

My punishment was somewhat harsher. Chuck dropped Kitty off and then he took me home. I remember being icy with fear. However, whatever Chuck did to me that afternoon—the details—are gone from my memory. They're completely blocked. I can't remember a word that he said. I don't remember him throwing a punch or kicking me, but I do know it was the worst beating I ever got. It was a day before I could walk again. And once I could walk, there was nowhere to go. What had been prison was now solitary confinement.

# seven

And so we got married.

Maybe.

I'm still not sure. It was that kind of a marriage. But I'll get to that in a minute.

Chuck Traynor spent much of that summer preparing for his upcoming trial on drug-smuggling charges. It seems that 400 pounds of marijuana—bales of pot wrapped around coke, hash, speed, LSD and assorted pills—had been dropped in a wooded area south of Miami, not far from the town of Homestead. Chuck and a friend had been caught carrying their bales to their cars, and a third confederate—this was Worth Devore—had gotten away uncaptured. The newspapers were all calling Worth "Mister X."

Since Chuck was not letting me out of his sight, I accompanied him on all his visits to his lawyer, Phil Mandina. Mandina seemed as slick as Chuck was crude—always immaculately dressed, flashy and glib. Mandina and Chuck had once been partners in a tiny airline that made daily runs to the Bahamas. Despite their many surface differences, the two men had much in common, as I was to learn.

"What're you doing for bread these days?" The lawyer

looked over at me, then up and down. "Back in the old business?"

"Back at the same old stand," Chuck said.

I disliked Phil Mandina at first sight. And, as time went on, this dislike was to ripen into hate. This was also my introduction to the legal system, and I didn't find much to like there either. We all knew, of course, that Chuck was guilty.

"Well, now," Mandina said, "what we're going to need here is a nice solid story. Fortunately, there's that one fellow who got away, this mysterious 'Mister X.' There's no doubt in our minds that he was there to get the contraband material. So, naturally, we'll do whatever is possible to make sure that Mister X gets the full blame."

I sat in on seven or eight meetings in Mandina's office. I was just another piece of furniture to them, part of the couch in the background, ignored, never part of the conversation, but always listening. Chuck was working out his alibi.

"Well, I believe I can tell you what we were doing out there on that day," Chuck said.

"I'm all ears," Mandina said.

"We were forming a sky-diving club," Chuck said. "You know, parachutes. And we were out there checking the fields to find a place for the sky-diving club to jump, a target area, you dig?"

"I dig," Mandina said. "That's not bad at all. A sky-diving club. Hmmm, not bad at all."

"Yeah, we were checking for a drop zone," Chuck said.

"I like it," Mandina said. "I *like* it. However, a sky-diving club would have to have members. You'll have to locate a few people who will testify that they were going to help you form your sky-diving club. Do you think you can swing that?"

"I don't see why not. Let me speak to a few guys."

"Right," Mandina said. "You speak to a few other charter members of this sky-diving club. Let's go over this again, Chuck. What were you doing out there in those fields?"

"We were checking it out."

"That's right," the lawyer said.

"We were walking over the terrain," Chuck said. "We wanted to be sure it was open enough, level enough, for a drop zone. We didn't want any of our members to break a leg."

"That's all well and good," Mandina said. "But when you were seen, you were carrying a bale of marijuana. Did you know that was marijuana?"

"Yeah, sure," Chuck said. "The thing is, we thought we better turn it right into the authorities."

"An excellent notion," Mandina said.

"Yeah, we had seen kids out there playing," Chuck said. "When we saw the stuff, just laying on the ground there, we decided we'd better turn it in before some of those kids found it."

During one of these meetings with the lawyer, Worth Devore—Mister X—came in for his briefing. When he was told that full blame for the operation was going to be placed on his shoulders, Worth had a few bad moments. He made them promise that he'd never be identified. At this point, Mandina seemed to notice my presence for the first time. He cupped his hand over Chuck's ear and whispered something.

"She stays," Chuck said. "She don't go nowhere without me."

"Well, there's no accounting for taste," Mandina said.

Most of Chuck's energy these days went toward finding a friend who would go to court and say he was a charter member of Chuck's sky-diving club. Although few of them were willing to risk a perjury charge, one friend, a fireman named Bob Phillips, went along with the story. This same Bob Phillips was later given a bit part in *Deep Throat*.

I couldn't imagine how Chuck was planning to pay his legal fees. I should have known better. Chuck never paid for anything himself. He and Mandina worked out a deal where I wound up paying for Chuck's defense. As a result of my automobile accident, I still had a case pending in New York and the lawyer who had been representing me was already receiving settlement offers. As payment for his case, Chuck gave Mandina the right to handle my case. The eventual settlement was more than $40,000 and was later used by Chuck and Mandina to form L. L. Enterprises. I never received any of the settlement money myself.

In their last meetings before the trial, Mandina and Chuck went over all the details. Worth Devore had been instructed not to go near the courthouse under any circumstances. Bob Phillips was ready to testify about the sky-diving club. And then Mandina put Chuck through his dress rehearsal, firing one question after another at him. When they were all through, I couldn't resist a comment.

"You're really going to tell the jury all that?" I asked. "You really think they're going to believe that?"

Mandina looked at me for a long moment.

"She knows a lot," he said.

"So?" Chuck said.

"She knows too much."

"So what can we do about that?"

"I'm not recommending anything," Mandina said. "I just think you should be aware of the fact that the D.A. would love to know what she knows. Incidentally, that's not entirely farfetched. Since she's not your wife, she could be called to testify against you."

Chuck thought about that but didn't respond immediately. It was not until the next day that I received my first serious proposal of marriage.

Marriage has always been important to me, perhaps too important. From when I was a small girl I had imagined what marriage would be like. That was all I ever expected from life—to get married to a good man, to have children, and to someday have a home of my own. When I got married, that was going to be it. Marriage is so important to me that I used to fantasize about all aspects of it—the proposal, the wedding night, the honeymoon. I had even imagined a man on his knees, asking for my hand. That's not quite the way it worked out.

"We're getting married tomorrow," Chuck said.

"No, we're not."

"Yeah, we are," Chuck said. "Only it's a long drive so you'll have to get your ass in gear early in the A.M."

"Chuck, no. We're not getting married."

"Did you say 'no' to me? Did I hear you say 'no' to me? Linda, I can't believe you'd be that reckless. I thought we had agreed that you'd never say 'no' to me."

"I'm not marrying you."

He hit me then and I cried out in pain. Then he started to choke me, and he didn't let go until I fell to the floor. Then the kicks started. This time I had the feeling that he wasn't going to stop in time, that he was going to go all the way and kill me.

The following morning we were married. Maybe. The reason I can't be sure is that I've tried to get my marriage certificate, but I've been told that the records for that month were destroyed. At this point I can't even be sure there was a genuine marriage.

If you ask me what date we were married, I couldn't tell you. There was no reason to remember the date; I knew that no anniversary would ever be celebrated. The only reason I know it was September is because it was shortly before Chuck's trial.

Chuck woke me up that day before dawn. It was a six-hour drive to the small town of Valdosta, Georgia, a long drive made longer still by being locked in a car with Chuck. Chuck was no longer content to get into a car and just drive somewhere. Now he had invented little games that helped him pass the time. One of his favorite games was to make me bare my breasts so that he could watch the reaction of passing truck drivers. And there was another game. Before stopping for gas, he would hike my skirt up above my hips and make me spread my legs. Then he'd ask the gas station attendant to please clean the windshield. This was all part of my day-by-day life and things didn't change just because it was my wedding day.

Chuck Traynor is surely one of the few men in the world who wouldn't consider going to a jewelry store to purchase his wedding ring. He went to a novelty shop. The ring he selected was plastic, one of those interlocking puzzle rings made from a dozen strangely shaped pieces. It set him back two dollars and change. For some reason, the ring did not seem at all inappropriate to the occasion.

When we arrived in Valdosta, we went to the town hall. We were ushered into the office of a Justice of the Peace. The office had high ceilings, narrow windows, a wall of legal books. The ceremony itself was the simple economy model: some quick "I do's" and no "Kiss the bride."

The only departure from form came when the Justice asked for the ring.

"What this?" he asked.

"It's a puzzle ring," Chuck explained.

"That's very cute," he said. "I've never seen one of these before."

As he handed the man the ring, Chuck dropped it, breaking it into its component parts. The justice spent several minutes trying to get the pieces back together but had to give up. I put it together and Chuck slipped it on my finger while the justice used the incident to make a point: "Well, I guess if you kids can keep this ring together, you'll be able to keep a marriage together."

Immediately after the ceremony, if that's the right word, Chuck drove me to a hotel in Valdosta. Just outside the hotel he asked a stranger if he would mind taking a photograph of us.

"Smile, babe," he said, "it's your wedding day."

He was having a grand old time. And he wouldn't let up. Once we were in the hotel room, he called his mother in North Carolina and told her that we had just tied the knot. She asked to speak to the bride.

"Best wishes!" she said. "I'm sure you'll both be as happy forever as you are now."

Although I was hoping for slightly more than that out of life, I did nothing to diminish her enthusiasm. Her excitement was transmitted very clearly over the phone and I didn't have the heart to ruin her day. Yes, I was certainly a lucky girl to "catch" her son. Yes, it had been a beautiful ceremony. Yes, I was sure we'd be very happy together.

When Chuck asked me whether I wanted to call my parents and share the good news with them, I declined the invitation.

The reality of my marriage, needless to say, fell somewhat short of my girlhood daydreams. That's one of the most important lessons I've learned from this entire experience: Never depend on fantasy. All my life I had a fantasy of a wedding day, a wedding night, a honeymoon, a handsome prince charming, a happy-ever-after.

Our wedding dinner? We went out to the local greasy spoon and had two cheeseburgers. Our wedding night? We came back to the room, turned on the television set and fell asleep. Sweet talk? This: "Now you'll never be able to testify against me. A wife can never testify against her husband. And another thing, you can never have me arrested—a wife can never charge her husband with a crime."

How could that be true? I've since discovered that there's no truth to it at all. But then—and this is just another indication of my gullibility—I accepted whatever Chuck said as the final word on the matter.

Our honeymoon was of a piece with the rest of the marriage. Needing some quick cash before his trial, Chuck decided to go to work for a few days. His cousin's husband, the owner of a large construction firm, offered Chuck work putting up sheetrock. As you might guess, that presented Chuck with a problem: How do you spend your days spackling sheetrock when you've got a brand new bride who wants to run away?

Chuck solved the problem in his own inimitable way. He asked his boss if he would mind guarding me while Chuck was working. In exchange for that, the boss could have sex with me whenever he wanted it. And that's how I spent my honeymoon, running my husband's house of prostitution while having periodic sex with his cousin's husband.

I was placing all of my hope in Chuck's upcoming trial. My freedom would surely come with Chuck's imprisonment, and that imprisonment seemed a certainty. The jury certainly would see through their little sky-diving story. And if someone is convicted of importing 400 pounds of pot, he doesn't get a slap on the wrist.

The trial lasted a week and, until Chuck took the stand, it went much the way I expected. Still, Chuck didn't seem overly worried as he sat there wearing his only decent clothes, a three-piece brown suit with a bright orange necktie.

Then Chuck took over—and I do mean took over. He has to be the greatest conman who ever lived. He had been caught red-handed with a bale of marijuana, and he told the jury he was just getting the stuff away from kids in the area. By the time he was through testifying about his sky-diving club, even I was looking for his parachute. After the not-guilty verdict, one of the jurors came over to Chuck.

"There just wasn't enough evidence against you," the juror said. "We couldn't be 100 percent sure you were guilty. But if you ever get into hot water again, we'll know."

Now they know.

As we were leaving the courtroom, I reached out and took a handful of Exhibit A—the marijuana—and stuck it in Chuck's jacket pocket. I know how irrational I was but I was half-hoping they'd search him on the way out of the courtroom, find the stuff, and try him all over again.

Chuck was on top of the world that afternoon, as up as I was down. He kept telling me about his glorious career as a high school debater, kept bragging about how he had turned a district attorney into a monkey.

I was depressed for several reasons. I was still not free of Chuck and, beyond that fact, I had just seen how easy it was for an accomplished liar to defeat the legal system in this country. It had been so easy for Chuck Traynor to manipulate the jury, the judge, the whole system. I had the feeling that there was nothing that could stop him now.

I was overcome with a feeling of hopelessness . . . of absolute depresion . . . of futility. Then, one more escape attempt. My older sister Jean had come with her little boy to Florida and they were staying at my parents' home.

Chuck arranged for a social outing, a day at the beach. But Jean must have picked up bad vibrations. We had been at the beach only a few minutes when she suddenly decided to go back to my parents' house. Chuck was angry but he went along with Jean.

Our first stop was Chuck's house. As Jean put on her clothes, I started rummaging through a bureau drawer. I saw something that sent chills through me. Photographs. Photograps of myself with another girl. Oh, God, what was her name again? Chicklet! Dozens of photos shot from every conceivable angle. Without saying a word, I swept all the photos into my purse and they remained there during the drive north to my parents' home. When we pulled up, I could see my father waiting for us beside the front door. Jean got out of the car and started walking toward the front door. I did the same.

"Where are you going?" Chuck said.

"Just a minute," I said. "You stay here."

Even as I stepped from the car, I had no clear idea of what I was doing. I turned away from Chuck and ignored what he was saying. My hands were trembling but once I started, there was no stopping. I followed my father and my sister into the house and the voice behind me, Chuck's voice, took on a pleading note.

"Yon can't leave me," he said. "You're my *wife*."

Until he said that, I didn't fully realize that I was leaving him. Not until I closed the front door of my father's house did it hit me. I was on one side of a closed door, and Chuck Traynor was on the other. As I leaned against the door, resting my back against it, my strength drained out of me.

Was it going to be this simple then? Was that even remotely possible? After everything, was I just going to be able to walk away from him?

"Oh?" My father noticed my presence. "Is something the matter?"

"Yes, everything's the matter. I've got to get away from Chuck. I don't ever want anything to do with him again."

"What's the matter, Linda?"

"I wouldn't even know how to tell you," I said. "You wouldn't believe it. You wouldn't believe any of it. There's just something wrong with Chuck. He's a very sick man. I don't ever want to go back to his house."

"How do you mean, sick?"

"He makes me do things. He makes me do things that aren't right. Sexual things."

I couldn't tell my father any more than that. I just couldn't. I didn't even know how to put it into words. And as I realized there was a closed door between the two worlds—two worlds that would never, ever understand each other—I felt a flood of emotions.

That afternoon my father took my sister and myself out to another beach. We were stretched out in the sun, just tanning ourselves, but I couldn't relax inside. I told myself that this was freedom and that I should enjoy it, but I kept opening my eyes and looking around. I expected to see Chuck coming for me. My father is a big man, well over six feet tall, but even his presence didn't reassure me. Chuck would come for me. I knew that. There was no way he would let me get away this easily. But when?

The next morning Jean opened up my purse and saw all those photographs. She woke me up.

"Linda, what're these?"

"That's my life with Chuck."

Jean went through the pictures methodically, stopping to study each one of them. I could see that she was going through changes.

"These pictures are *awful!*" she said. "You've got to get

rid of them. If Mommy ever sees these pictures, she'll die."

We tore the photographs into small pieces and took turns flushing them down the toilet. I felt better, much better, as I watched the pieces swirl away. But I knew that I wouldn't be able to get Chuck out of my life and out of my mind that easily.

Later, as both my folks went off to work, Jean and I stayed home together. I had to make plans. Chuck knew where I was. Therefore, I had to go somewhere else. I had to get out of Chuck's range. But where? I was stumped. This was the only place I seemed to have any protection at all. And how could I even get away from there? I imagined Chuck outside, still in the neighborhood, hiding behind a bush or a telephone pole, just waiting for me to try and slip away.

By late afternoon I still hadn't come up with a specific plan of action. All I knew was that I would have to get away from Florida. Just before dinner my mother said she wanted to talk to me.

"Chuck has been calling all day," she said. "I've talked to him a few times now and all I know for sure is that he really loves you."

"Mother, you don't know what you're talking about."

"Oh, you never think that I know what I'm talking about," she said. "I've been married a good long time, longer than you've been alive, and after all this time I guess I know a thing or two about husbands and wives. You don't want to forget that he's your husband and you're his wife. No matter what little difficulties you've been having, you should be able to work them out."

"Little difficulties? *Little* difficulties!"

"Chuck told me everything," my mother said. "He told me enough so that I know this is just a lovers' quarrel."

All day I had been thinking about how I could tell my parents what was going on in my life. I felt that I should break it to them gently. Well, all those plans just flew out the window. I laid the situation flat-out, using the bluntest words that I knew.

"Mom, Chuck has beaten me bloody," I began. "He has held a gun to my head and made me do awful things. He has forced me to have sex with women and other men. And now he is talking about making me have sex with animals. He has made me pose for dirty pictures and he is turning me into a prostitute. He is always threatening to kill me. He has even threatened to kill you and Daddy."

"But, Linda, he's your *husband*."

"Mother, you're not hearing me. You're not hearing a word that I'm saying."

"Well, let me tell you something else," she said. "Chuck happens to be on his way over here right this minute. He should be here any time now, and I want you to remember one thing. He's your husband and you're his wife."

. "I've got to get out of here. I've got to go."

"Linda, he'll be here in just a second."

*"Mom!"*

"He *promised* me! He promised me that he would never make you do anything wrong again."

I got up to go.

"Mom, you just don't understand a thing."

"Oh, yes, I do," she said. "Chuck told me everything. He also told me that he was sorry for anything bad that happened, and he doesn't know what came over him."

The doorbell was ringing. My mother opened the door and Chuck was there, all dressed up the way he had dressed for his trial. He smiled as my mother led the two of us into a room.

"I'm leaving the two of you alone to talk things out," she said.

Chuck and I were alone then. Well, not quite alone. My sister's little boy came into the room and starting playing with his toy trucks. Chuck showed me the bulge in his trouser pocket.

"I'm going to shoot this little boy in his fucking head," he said, still smiling. "If you don't get up and come along with me, this little boy will die first."

"My father will—"

"Your father will die next," he said. "When he comes through that door, he will get a bullet between his eyes. Then your mother and your cunt-sister, I'll blow them all away. Maybe then, when they're all fucking dead, you'll decide to come along with me. Maybe not."

I followed him then through the rest of the house and out the front door. My mother was beaming.

"See, Linda," she said, "I knew you two kids could work things out."

People always ask me why I never called the police. It seemed to me that the system would never work for me, only against me. Then, too, I believed Chuck's totally absurd story that a wife could not charge a husband with a crime. The one time I did bring in the police—this was much later on—I discovered that that totally absurd story could also be true.

Now I was Chuck Traynor's prisoner and Phil Mandina's meal ticket. Since he would be handling my case up in New York, Mandina suddenly decided that I was socially acceptable. When he took his girlfriend Barbara up to North Carolina to look over a piece of investment property, we were invited along for the ride.

We flew up in the lawyer's private plane, a twin-engined Cessna. Barbara was a beautician, a little on the plump side, with dirty blonde hair. Apparently beauticians didn't spend much time working on their own hair. But at least she was a nice dresser. Barbara wore matching outfits or cocktail dresses while I was wearing jeans and insulated thermal shirts. Mandina favored vested suits, and Chuck looked like a refugee from an army-navy store window.

Although Chuck and I were never well dressed, it only became a problem when we were out of our element. And this weekend we were in a fancy resort hotel filled with potential investors from all over the country. I felt self-conscious from the beginning, and Chuck didn't help matters at all when he gave me my standard public-appearance briefing.

"Listen, there's going to be a lot of people down there for dinner," he said, "and I don't want to see you drifting away. Don't go to the john without me; don't even fucking ask. If you've got to go, we'll come back up to the room here. I don't want to see you talking to no strangers. Don't say nothing to no one. Some clown asks you a question, you don't know shit."

This speech, with minor variations, was given to me whenever we were to be in the company of strangers. I must've come off like the world's dumbest human being. I was allowed to say, "This food tastes nice" or "The weather is nice today" but that was about the extent of my social conversation. I've got to wonder what other people thought. And what on earth did they think when they saw me asking Chuck's permission to go to the bathroom?

After the dinner that first night, the four of us—Chuck, myself, Mandina and Barbara—got together in one of the bedrooms. The two men were drinking Scotch and passing around joints. Then they got into a bragging contest; they each claimed to be the world's greatest hypnotist. Mandina said he could hypnotize Barbara into doing anything he wanted. Chuck told them how he had hypnotized me into the deep-throat techniques.

"She can take the whole thing in her mouth," he said. "She can swallow the whole thing."

"Oh, Phil tried to get me to do that," Barbara giggled. "But I could never manage it. I think Phil's just too much man for me."

This was the level of conversation that night. And before we were through, the two men decided to demonstrate their prowess as hypnotists. Mandina put Barbara under and gave her a post-hypnotic suggestion: "When you wake up, you are going to be very thirsty. You're going to feel like you're in the middle of the desert, and you're going to run into the bathroom for a drink of water."

After awakening, Barbara fluttered her eyes a couple of times and then made a dash for the bathroom. She immediately realized what had happened and she said, "Oh, Phil, you did it to me again."

Then Chuck hypnotized me. Chuck had a sure-fire way of telling when I was really hypnotized and when I was faking it so there was nothing to do but allow myself to be hypnotized. Chuck's post-hypnotic suggestion took a somewhat different course, one more in keeping with his personality.

"When you come to, you are going to take off all your clothes," he said. "You will get undressed and you will get turned on when you look at Barbara. Then you are going over to Barbara and you are going to undress her. And then you'll make love to Barbara. All she'll have to do is touch you and you'll come."

When he took me out of hypnosis, I was in a cold sweat. Sometimes I was able to remember everything Chuck said to me when I was under. Some of his suggestions I was powerless to resist, and some I just wouldn't do. He once told me to make love to a dog and I wouldn't do that; another time he told me I would have an orgasm during oral sex with a man, and that didn't happen, although it was eventually the entire plot of *Deep Throat*.

To protect myself from a later beating—and Chuck would be furious with me if I didn't follow his post-hypnotic suggestions—I would always play along at least part of the way. So I began by taking off my clothes. I took off all my clothes and stopped. In a way I was playing along with Chuck, and in a way I wasn't. All three of them were staring at me, waiting for the rest of it. And then I undressed Barbara. It was a strange sensation. As I was doing it, I became more and more scared. I knew what they were waiting for, and I didn't know how far I was going to go. If that sounds confused, it should. I *was* confused.

We were both naked then and we were sitting on the carpet together. I knew what was supposed to happen next. I was expected to put my arms around Barbara and start making love to her. But that didn't happen. I couldn't go that far.

There's one thing about all that hypnotism that really scares me. Someday I'm going to sit down with a psychiatrist and get everything out. There are whole days, groups of days, when I don't remember a thing. Sometimes I'd wake up and have to ask what day of the week it was. The things I can remember are so horrible, I wonder what happened on those days that I can't remember. The idea of finding out scares me, but the idea of never finding out scares me even more.

Repeated exposures to Phil Mandina didn't make him any more likable. Still, Chuck continued to bring the four of us together after our return to Miami. Now our meetings took place on Mandina's houseboat. Chuck kept telling me I had to get something going with Barbara, or else.

I warned Barbara about this: "There's something crazy about Chuck. He's always trying to get me to do weird things. Now he's mad at me because I haven't been coming on with you at all."

"Oh, Phil's just like that, too," Barbara said. "He's always after me to do crazy things. The only reason I do them is it makes him so happy."

On this particular night, the two men were inventing contests. They decided they would go down on the two women and whoever made the woman come first would be the winner. Chuck would go down on Barbara and Mandina would go down on me. I could've told Mandina to save his energy, but there would've been no discouraging the two of them. It finally ended with Barbara noisily claiming victory.

One game led to another. This time the boys decided on a reversal: Barbara went down on Chuck and I took care of Mandina. Although I despised the lawyer, it had to be done, and done well. Chuck was still upset that I wasn't coming on with Barbara so I had to make up for that. If I didn't satisfy Mandina, then I'd be in for a beating. My thinking: if I do this well, then I'll be covered with Chuck for the evening. This was the minimum I could get away with. I often thought in those terms, the minimum I could get away with.

So although I hated Phil Mandina, I did what I had to do.

Often, when I was in a situation like this, I would get some small revenge by "accidentally" biting the man. This time I couldn't take that chance.

Mandina was satisfied. Months later he called me in Hollywood and told me that I should give Barbara special deepthroat instructions over the telephone—she was trying to do it right then but without success. I could hear her giggling in the background.

Some people don't understand how you can have sex with someone you hate. I kept looking for ways to make it possible. I was smoking more and more pot. Later, when I discovered a pain-killer called *Percodan*, I'd really load up on it and become totally numb to what was happening to me. But there were some pains that *Percodan* didn't make go away.

At the end of our first summer together, Chuck announced that he was taking his bride on a little trip. We were off to Aspen, Colorado. I had learned not to press Chuck for details but this time he volunteered a little information. A friend of his had just started a bar in Aspen and he needed a girl to work as a go-go dancer and after-hours hooker.

I no longer even reacted to bulletins like these. Whatever Chuck told me to do, I did. No questions asked. How he had accomplished this, I don't know. He was constantly belittling me, humiliating me, and degrading me. The beatings were endless. I was being hypnotized several times a week. And the changes in my personality were not subtle ones.

I was no longer experiencing things that made me feel good or bad. I felt as though my self had been taken away from me. I was not a person anymore. I was a robot, a vegetable, a wind-up toy, a fucking-and-sucking doll. I had become someone else's thing. If I didn't do . . . whatever— I got beaten. So I simply did it. Whatever.

During the long drive toward Aspen, Chuck kept thinking up new things for me to do. New car games. And I was his biggest toy. If I told you some of the games, you'd have trouble believing them. At least I hope you would. One example: He would buy Red Hots, those tiny cinnamon candies that kids love, and he would stick a handful of them in my vagina and watch me squirm as we drove along. If we happened to run out of his precious Red Hots, he'd yell at me until we found a store that carried them.

Since we were low on funds, Chuck decided that we'd have to earn money on our way to Aspen. How would we do that? Chuck outlined his plan to me in a small town in Arkansas, a town too small to have its own police department but just large enough to support a haberdashery. Chuck pulled our car up in front of the haberdashery and looked in the window. It was empty except for two salesmen.

"Go in there and speak to those two guys," Chuck told me. "Tell them you'll give them a blow job for $10.00. No, wait, let's start off with twenty. If they don't go for that, tell them you really need the bread bad so you'll do it for ten."

I got out of the car and started walking toward the store. Chuck rolled down the window.

"That's ten *each*," he said.

As I walked into the store, the two men straightened up behind the counter and smiled a nice, friendly, small-town smile. I took a last look back toward the street. Chuck had gotten out of the car and was now pretending to window-shop while watching me closely. What to do? Suddenly I remembered the trouble my father always had finding the right size shirt.

"I'd like to look at a shirt," I said, "but it has to have very long arms."

"How long?" one of the salesman asked. "We carry most sizes up to a seventeen neck and thirty-six-inch sleeves."

"This is a fifteen neck," I said, "and a forty-inch sleeve."

"Forty inches We don't have anything like that."

He was shaking his head no, which was just what I wanted. Then the second salesman started to laugh. Evidently I had just given them a shirt size that would have been perfect for an orangutan. And this is what Chuck saw through the

window—one salesman shaking his head no, the second salesman laughing at me.

"Well, thanks anyway."

I turned on my heels and walked out of the store, letting
the door slam behind me. I started to tell Chuck how I'd
been turned down and he interrupted me.

"Save it," he said. "I saw it all. These fucking hillbillies
probably never saw a real live cunt before."

I used that same ploy whenever we traveled. No matter
what kind of store Chuck sent me into, I asked for something
that was both too large and purple, something outlandish
enough to get a quick no. Chuck was confused by all the
rejections.

"You gotta be doing something wrong," he said. "You're
no fucking good at all. You can't even give a hillbilly shop-
keeper a fucking hard-on."

I almost smiled. Almost. This was one of the few times
that I got the better of Chuck. It may not seem like such a
big deal to you, but to me it was a win. I couldn't escape but
I could maneuver a bit within the system. Anytime I got the
better of Chuck—and just conning him was enough—I felt a
small flash of pleasure.

During the long drive, Chuck seemed to have just one
thing on his mind. He kept talking about a little detour we
were going to make, a detour to Mexico. "Wait 'till we get
to Juarez," he'd say. Or, "Only 650 miles to Juarez." Or
"Once we're in Juarez, we'll be able to pick up some easy
money."

I didn't bother asking what was waiting for us in Juarez.
From the way he was going on, it was not something I wanted
to hear. I also suspected that he'd get to the point before
we drove too much farther.

"I hope you like donkeys," he said.

"Donkeys are fine."

"There's no fucking reason you should like donkeys," he
said. "It's just that it'd be a good thing if you did like donkeys
is all. It'd be better for you."

"What would be better if I liked donkeys?"

"Donkeys'd be better," he said.

"*Why* would it be better if I liked donkeys?"

"Because you're going to be fucking them in Juarez," he came to the point. "That's what I've been telling you, that's the reason we're going to Juarez. To fuck donkeys."

He had to be kidding. Didn't he? His eyes were off the road and on my face. Evidently I didn't register sufficient shock because he felt compelled to describe all the wonders waiting for us in Juarez. He talked about an arena similar to the pit used for a cockfight—hundreds of men sitting around a ring, yelling out their wagers. In the middle of the ring, naked women and a donkey. The men would be betting on the various women. Specifically on how many centimeters of donkey penis each woman would be able to contain in her vagina.

"You're *made* for this contest," Chuck said. "I'm telling you, you'll clean up. Shee-yit, the last chick I brought to Juarez made us three thou and she was nothin'."

This was surely just another story, another of Chuck's little on-the-road entertainments. However, there were too many details. If it was all make-believe, he had given it a lot of thought.

"The chicks go in one at a time," he was saying. "And the crowd cheers, just like when prizefighters come into a ring. And then they strap the chick up on this contraption and then they bring out their trained donkey and they lead the donkey right into the fucking cunt."

"You're lying!" I said. "How could a donkey do anything with a woman?"

"Oh, he gets a little fucking help," Chuck said, obviously pleased that I was finally reacting. "They've got to point him right, you dig? Sometimes the chick gets ripped up a little—I'm telling you, you haven't lived 'till you've seen one of those donkey dongs. Those suckers are *huge!* And the guys are all bidding like they're at some fucking auction—'I'll bet a thousand on the redhead,' like that."

"That would kill a woman."

"Nah, they got the medicos right there," Chuck said. "If the bleeding gets too bad, they unstrap the chicks and give them medical assistance right on the spot. Some of those chicks are really hemorrhaging, too."

I couldn't tell when Chuck was telling the truth. But I was *scared*. As the miles piled up, he got more and more graphic. He seemed to like the word "hemorrhage" because he used it a lot. At night I went to sleep dreaming about women bleeding. I also dreamt about animals making love to women—but those images were fuzzy. How could they do it? *Could* they do it?

Maybe all of this was one of Chuck's inventions but I have never prayed so hard in my life: *Dear God, please don't let us get to Juarez, Mexico; please stop us from going to Juarez.*

And God answered my prayers one night outside of Little Rock, Arkansas. All of a sudden Chuck's little Volkswagen just took off. It had been hit from behind by a station wagon driven by a drunk. We swerved to the right, then to the left, then off into a ditch and over onto our side. The next thing I knew, truck drivers were crawling all over the car, looking for a way to lift us out. I heard one of them say, "Well, that little car has had it."

Thank God! I knew that God had done it. The automobile accident was definitely God answering my prayers. Maybe not verbatim, maybe not giving me everything that I wanted, but at least protecting me.

From what?

From being fucked by a donkey in Juarez, Mexico.

# *eight*

Juarez was now out of the question, and Little Rock definitely *was not* Chuck's kind of a town. So we got a ride to New York which definitely *was* Chuck's kind of town.

We couldn't afford an apartment in the city itself, but Chuck found us a place on the other side of the Hudson—in Jersey City, New Jersey. After putting up a month's security and a month's rent, Chuck had less than $50.00 left. He invested some of this in purchasing every sex tabloid published in New York City.

Once he had the newspapers, Chuck went through the classified ads, looking for suitable employment for me. These were not your ordinary *Help Wanted* ads. In fact, I read the same classified ads that Chuck was reading, and I couldn't understand what they were talking about. They were written in some kind of code. They used phrases like "English Leather Fanciers" and "French Instruction" and "Greek Spoken Here" and "TV Specialists." Chuck knew exactly what they all meant.

"This is some town!" he said. "They get away with stuff here they haven't even thought of back in Miami."

As he went through the newspaper ads, Chuck circled

telephone numbers. His first calls were all to S&M—sadism and masochism—numbers, but these calls were for his own general information. When he began looking for employment for me, he called the numbers in the "Models Wanted" columns.

"Well, Babe, we're back in business," he said. "Your old man has everything under control."

It was not all that simple. My career as a topless dancer, for example, lasted less than one night. We were racing from one address to another in the midtown area of New York City, and one of our stops was a small bar off 42nd Street. It was like a little auditorium with thirty or forty seats. There were girls dancing, and, between sets, they hustled drinks from the customers.

After speaking to the club manager for a few minutes, Chuck told me to go upstairs and put on a G-string.

"This could be easy money," Chuck said. "So you're up on a stage bare-assed for a couple of hours every night, so what's the big deal? This way you'll be able to work with photographers during the day and dance topless at night. Just until we find something more steady."

That prospect—"something more steady"—sent a small shudder through me. But, in truth, the whole topless bar scene was as embarrassing as anything I've ever done. I went into a small room, took off my clothes and put on the G-string while one of the dancers was giving me advice.

"Listen, honey, there's nothing to this," she was saying. "Just dance up close to the end of the stage and let your tits hang down so the creeps can almost reach them. Then, when you're spreading your legs, just lift your G-string a little, you know what I'm saying?"

Waiting to go down the stairs and onto the stage, I could hear the manager introducing me.

"What we got here—for your entertainment and enjoyment—a brand new star, fresh from Florida and points west, about to grace our stage here for the first time . . ."

There had been no chance to watch the other dancers, so

I had no idea what was expected of me. Suddenly, in front of dozens of glittering eyes, I was on a stage—wearing a piece of string and feeling as stupid as I've ever felt—doing some regular disco dancing. And the customers made no attempt to conceal their feelings. Those who weren't yawning, were hooting at me. I finished a couple of numbers, then made a dash for the upstairs dressing room. Followed by Chuck. Followed by the manager.

"What're you two trying to do, put all my customers to sleep?"

The upshot was that the brand new star, fresh from Florida and points west, got no pay at all for her show-business debut. Chuck was quick to assure me that there'd be many other opportunities in the near future, and he was right. New York City was truly the land of opportunity for Chuck.

There were hundreds of people who made their livings by peddling sex in New York. What was amazing to me was how quickly one got to know them all. They were all links on the same chain; you met one person, and he passed you along to the others. The still photographers knew the club owners who knew the madams who knew the eight-milli-meter directors who knew the peep-show kingpins who knew the adult book store owners and so on. I swear, before that first week was out, Chuck Traynor managed to meet almost every prominent pervert in New York. My life was a succession of job interviews.

One of those first interviews was with a whore named Xaviera Hollander.

Although Xaviera was not yet famous as "the happy hooker," hers was no nickel-and-dime operation. The uni-formed doorman at her East Side apartment building informed us that Miss Hollander would be detained for a few moments and asked us to be good enough to wait in the lobby.

And this is where I met Xaviera Hollander. My first reac-tion to her was that New York City must be pretty hard up if someone who looked like her could become a successful madam. She was fat. Her hair was dirty, all caked with grease. She had piled the makeup on a face that needed more than mere makeup. We followed her to the elevator and on up to her apartment.

"Tom sent us over," Chuck said. "He thought that maybe you could use my old lady here in your operation."

"No, I don't think so." Xaviera looked me over like a butcher inspecting a side of beef. "She's too skinny. She's not my type at all."

"She's a good hooker . . ."

"I've already got enough brown-haired girls," Xaviera said. "Maybe if she was a redhead . . ."

"She could be a redhead," Chuck said. "No problem."

Before responding, Xaviera went to pick up a ringing telephone. The call was from a publisher and they were talking about some book that was about to come out under Xaviera's name. While she was talking, Chuck whispered to me.

"Come on with her a little."

"No way."

"Tell her you'd like to give her a little free sample of what you can do," he said. "It won't kill you. And ask her if she's got any dildoes around. Tell her you can show her some new things with dildoes."

"No."

Xaviera returned. She was looking at our clothes and was more amused than impressed. We were in our usual outfits: blue jeans, waterproof boots, and army jackets.

"Those clothes are awful," Xaviera said. "You know, my clients are astronauts and judges. They take my girls to formal parties. They don't want girls who look like hippies, they want nice girls."

I began to wonder what kind of a hooker ever dressed the way I was dressed. Chuck, realizing that this prospect was slipping away from us, went to his hard sell.

"Linda's not a typical hooker," he said. "She could show you—why don't you let her give you a little sample."

"I'm not talking about what she *does*," Xaviera said. "I'm talking about the way she looks. My girls have nice clothes, a lot of class. They're able to sit down and have dinner with the mayor or the governor."

"Yeah, but not all your tricks are big shots," Chuck said. "You must get your share of freaks and guys who go for the far-out stuff. Linda could do them."

"No, I don't think so."

All the way to our next appointment, this one with a Swedish madam named Milka, Chuck yelled at me. He said that Xaviera was right, I was too skinny. He could never make up his mind about that. One day he'd yell at me for being too skinny, the next for being too fat. Then he went back to his favorite theme: I wasn't freaky enough. If I had been more freaky, I would have come on with Xaviera Hollander and gotten the job that way. I crept into my shell and closed it tightly behind me.

Xaviera's rejection didn't bother me in the least. In fact, being turned down by her was a compliment in a way.

The second madam, Milka, was at least nice looking. She was with a friend, Martin, and they both scrutinized me, much the way Xaviera had, but they didn't come to a quick decision. Chuck decided to help them make up their minds: "Why doesn't Linda give Martin a free sample, see what he thinks."

Martin led me over to a double bed in the far corner of the room. Fish netting, draped like curtains over the bed, was all the privacy we had. Something that I can't explain hit me then. While the act was happening, while his thing was in my mouth, I started crying. It was as if my whole life had come down to this moment and this act—sucking off a stranger—and I couldn't hold back the sadness. Martin eased away from me.

"You don't really want to do this?" he whispered.

"No."

"Then cool it," he said. "You're not into this kind of thing; you shouldn't be doing it. Come on, Linda, calm down now, nothing is going to happen. We'll wait here a few minutes and then we'll go back out there."

There was no more conversation. Martin rubbed my back soothingly while we waited for the proper amount of time to pass, then we went back to Chuck and the madam.

"She's really fantastic," Martin said. "She's the greatest. Chuck was right."

"What'd I tell you?" Chuck said.

"Yeah," Martin said, "I never had a blow job like that."

Somehow, although he was saying just what Chuck wanted to hear, he was also letting Milka know that something was not quite right here. She listened to him and then turned to us.

"Well, Linda, if we can use you, we'll get in touch with you."

In other words: Don't call us, we'll call you. Which was fine with me, but not so fine with Chuck.

About this same time, one of Chuck's former hookers in Miami showed up and moved in with us. Brandy, a still fresh-looking eighteen-year-old girl with long brown hair, had only worked as a prostitute for five or six weeks. In fact, she was still involved in a mental debate: Should she become a full-time hooker or should she give it up and marry her high-school sweetheart and start a family? I told her she was crazy to come back to Chuck and the business, but she only laughed at that.

Brandy and I had done several tricks together in Florida, and our first job in New York was for a still photographer. This was in a studio that was used exclusively for sado-masochistic photos: chains hanging from walls, strange medieval torture devices, a full selection of whips, a jumbo-sized bottle of Heinz ketchup.

Brandy and I stripped down, then took turns pretending to whip and torture each other. It was all so absurd. What kind of a man would get turned on by seeing a picture of a naked woman with ketchup smeared across her back?

From still photographs it was a short distance to the world of movies. Just across the street, as a matter of fact, to a studio where they shot eight-millimeter movies for the peep-show trade. The thought of making a movie really bothered me. When they were taking still photographs, you could always stop whatever you were doing and take a breather. You didn't have to act as though you were enjoying every minute of it. I had no idea how I was going to fake it long enough for them to shoot a movie.

"We'll just give it a try," Brandy said. "What's the big deal? We've done plenty of tricks for twenty—why not do a movie for a hundred?"

"It's no big deal," Chuck said. "When we get there, you two just do like the man tells you. Tonight, we'll have a little dress rehearsal."

Chuck's idea of a dress rehearsal was for Brandy and myself to have sex together while he watched. He was always trying to push the two of us together. He would get the three of us in bed together, and he'd begin by taking my hand and putting it on Brandy's breast. Then he would take Brandy's hand and put it inside of me. Brandy got no more pleasure from any of this than I did. But she was like me in one crucial respect: She went along with it.

While Chuck was brutal to me, he was nice with Brandy. In fact, I never saw him rough up another woman. Maybe because other women would not have taken it. The way I see things now, I was still a baby. He had taken me directly from the cradle to the whorehouse, and brutality was the only thing that kept me there.

Well, I had been involved with Brandy for the benefit of tricks, and I didn't see anything in the movie that was going to be any different. So I went along with it.

Those first eight-millimeter movies were shot in a loft near 48th Street and Broadway by a man named Tom. The bathroom sink was filthy. The rooms were filled with odd pieces of furniture covered by sheets. The floors had never been mopped and your feet turned black just walking on them. The people who made filthy movies always seemed to live in filth.

Tom introduced us to our co-star for the day, a nice-looking young man named Rob. I wound up making a half-dozen of the eight-millimeter movies with Rob, including some with his wife, Cathy. The first time I met Rob, I wondered how this could be. Here's this real doll—he was *adorable!*— tall and blond and cute. How could a guy who looked like that do what he did for a living? What problems did he have to get into something like this? I will never understand that.

The director, Tom, told Brandy and me to take off our clothes and lie on the bed. He told us to lie there naked and be laughing and talking together and then to start kissing each other.

All right, I had to kiss her. Instead of moving right along, as the director wanted, I kind of hesitated at this point. I hated to move right along, even though that was the only way to get through these jobs. Then, when Brandy and I were supposedly getting into it, a guy appeared in the scene.

This was Rob. Brandy and I pretended to be surprised to see him: First we feigned embarrassment, then we pretended to be happy to have a fresh body. This was the whole story of the movie. Rob took off his clothes, and then, while the two of us kissed him all over, he got sexually aroused. Oh, God, it seemed so absurd while we were doing it; even more absurd now when I'm remembering it.

Maybe I should've been used to all this by now. But I wasn't. Whenever it happened—whenever something like this was coming down—I felt disgusted all over again. That never changed. There were always tears in my eyes and a lump in my throat, and if Chuck saw that—if he even saw me looking moody—there would be a certain punishment.

In time I learned a thing or two. I learned a false smile was a lot better than a real beating, so I'd just paste that smile on my face no matter what was happening. I also learned that if I didn't get into it quickly, then I'd have to be at it longer. So I got right into it, did it quickly, smiled all the time and got it over with. Later, in the shower, I would tell myself that it hadn't really happened.

Tom and Rob introduced Chuck to the other people who were making eight-millimeter movies. The first film was actually a fairly straight one, if you can believe that. Tom did relatively normal films, but the same couldn't be said for my next director, Bob Wolf. That first film was plenty disgusting, but at least no one was urinating on anyone.

I'm being serious about this. Bob Wolf referred to one of our eight-millimeter epics as "the piss movie." This is one that I made with Rob and his wife, Cathy. The movie began with what I suppose is a fairly traditional porn opening— the old girl-meets-girl-meets-boy formula. At any rate, the three of us were in bed together and after we had done everything that three people could do to each other sexually, the director decided that the movie would come to a socko finish with the actors urinating on each other.

You may wonder how they introduced this scene smoothly into the movie, or how they explained it in terms of character motivation. Well, that kind of thought never occurred to anyone working on an eight-millimeter movie. All I know is that the director had about five minutes of film left to shoot when the inspiration hit him.

"All right, Rob," Bob Wolf said, "you lie down over there on that rubber sheet. And Cathy, you and Linda come over here and piss on him."

I blinked at that. But I wasn't all that surprised. That was a measure of how far I had gone in less than a year. Piss on him? Sure, why not? But as it turned out, it was not that easy to do. Cathy was the first to try.

"I can't do it," she said.

"Oh you can't?" Wolf seemed upset by her lack of professionalism. "Well, fine, if you can't be the pisser, you can be the pissee. Cathy, you lie down, and Rob, you and Linda piss on her."

This kind of stuff didn't bother Rob and Cathy too much.

They had made so many eight-millimeter movies, both with each other and with other people, that life held no surprises for them. So now Cathy was lying down on the rubber sheet and she was told to act ecstatic, as though this was bringing her much more satisfaction than regular love-making. However, neither Rob nor I were able to play our parts properly.

"Cut!" Now Wolf was livid. "All right, all right, let's send out for some beer."

I've heard how some Method actors prepare for their big scenes, concentrating intensely on character motivation, drawing on a reservoir of past experiences and so on. The three of us prepared for our big scene by chug-a-lugging six-packs of beer.

It was so insane. Even when my mind was numb to everything, my body seemed to know it was insane. When it came my turn to urinate on Cathy, I couldn't do it. Even with a bellyful of beer, I couldn't urinate on another human being.

"Cut!" Wolf said. "All right, Linda, you're having such trouble, you get down there on the sheet and they'll piss on you."

"Wait a minute," I said. "Give me another chance."

All of a sudden it became easier. I was standing there, still aware of the sheer insanity of it all, but doing it nonetheless. I guess I was still strong enough so that I would rather piss on than be pissed upon.

And that was the whole movie. Really disgusting. People are so sick; they actually sit back, watching and enjoying these things. I still don't understand it. And whenever I think of Rob and Cathy, it seems even sicker. I cannot understand being married and having a nice apartment and going out every day to make porno films. I cannot comprehend that—let alone comprehend why you would let yourself get pissed on.

# *nine*

———————

I suppose my rise in the film world might accurately be described as meteoric. One day I was making photographs with ketchup smeared on my back, and three weeks later I was asked to play the lead in what was to become one of the biggest money-making films of all time. I had known Chuck Traynor less than a year and he had driven me into depths I hadn't known were there. However, all things considered, I shouldn't have been surprised when one porno director put the question to me one morning.

"We've been thinking of making a dog movie," he said. "Would that interest you?"

"No."

On those few occasions when I was asked to participate, my quick and natural response was, "No." I said no before I even considered the question. A dog movie? A *dog* movie? A dog *movie?* I knew they weren't thinking about *Rin Tin Tin* or *Lassie Come Home*. They were undoubtedly considering a girl-meets-dog movie.

"There'd be a lot of money in it," he said. "A lot more than usual."

"I'm not interested," I said. "I'm afraid of dogs."

Chuck overheard the conversation and accurately judged

my feelings on the subject. I'm not sure whether that was what intrigued him or whether it was just the prospect of making a little more money than usual, but that night back in our Jersey City apartment he informed Brandy and myself that the following morning we would be making a movie with a dog.

"No dice," Brandy said. "I won't do anything like that."

"Sure you will," Chuck said. "It's no big deal. There's nothing to it, you'll see."

"I'm not doing anything with a dog," Brandy said, "except maybe walk it or feed it."

"Oh, yeah, you are." This was the first time I ever saw Chuck talk tough to Brandy. "I promised them two chicks, and I'm going to fucking deliver two. They're paying $150 each—hey, that doesn't sound so bad, does it?"

"They can shove their bread," Brandy said.

"Well, we'll just see about that," Chuck said. "We'll see who shoves what where tomorrow morning first thing."

I was behind Brandy 100 percent but I couldn't say a word. If I had told Chuck what Brandy just did, I'd be near dead from the beating. In New York, Chuck had been as brutal as ever with me. I see now that he didn't always hit me out of genuine anger; it was his way of keeping me scared and under control. But when he was angry, it was far worse.

That night Chuck was taking me over to Manhattan to meet another moviemaker. Before we left, Brandy and I had a little talk.

"Linda, I've got to tell you something. I'm not going to be around here for any dog tomorrow."

"What're you going to do?"

"I'm splitting," she said. "By the time you guys get back from the city, I'll be long gone."

"Please don't do that," I said. "If there's two of us there tomorrow, we don't have to do anything. If it's just me—"

"I'm sorry, honey," Brandy said, "but I'm not hanging around for some goddamned dog. I wasn't sure whether or not I even wanted this life, but now I'm pretty sure. This ain't for me. Your old man is really far out."

"I need you."

"Linda, honey," she said, "I've got to split."

And split she did. When we got back to the apartment that night, Brandy was gone and all of her clothes were gone, too. There was no note of explanation. Chuck was furious. He went banging from one end of the apartment to the other, turning over furniture, emptying drawers, shouting what he was going to do to Brandy when he found her.

I didn't say a word, just tried to keep out of his way. I particularly did not say anything about the dog movie the next morning. But that night I dreamed about dogs. When Chuck had told me about the donkey, I was never sure whether he was goofing or not. This time I knew he was serious.

There had only been one dog in my family. When I was eleven years old, I had a puppy that I used to take for walks on a leash. Whenever we went for a walk, the other dogs in the neighborhood would come and pick on the two of us. I can still see them growling and barking and baring their teeth. That's the way I was seeing them in my dreams that night. As for a dog having sex with a woman, that seemed impossible. There was no way—just no way—that I was going to let one of them near me.

The following morning I didn't say anything to Chuck. I knew the only time to tell him was when other people were around. Witnesses. There would be a beating, I knew that much, but it would be easier on me if other people were nearby. For once, the prospect of a beating was not the worst alternative. Any beating, no matter how severe, would be better than being raped by a dog.

Our destination that morning was a studio down in the East Village. A large room . . . the usual clutter . . . the double bed . . . the movie lights . . . the cameras . . . the director, Robert Wolf—fat and greasy and black-haired.

"You said *two* chicks," he said to Chuck. "Where's the other one."

"She split," Chuck explained.

"Jesus Christ! Well, we'll just have to make do." As he turned toward me, he tried to strike an ingratiating note. "Well, you're looking good this morning, Linda. And I want you to know how much I appreciate your going through with this."

It was time to speak up. "I'm not going to do it."

"What?"

"I'm not letting any dog near me."

"What is this bullshit?" He stared at Chuck who was glaring at me. "Chuck, I can't bring this joker all the way down here again and tell him it's not going to come off. I can't have that kind of bullshit. This guy is coming all the way down here with this dog—and I'm supposed to tell him to forget it? Do you know how many times I've had him come down here with his fucking dog?"

"Don't worry about a thing," Chuck said. "Linda'll be okay. I'll speak to her."

As Chuck led me out of the studio to the hallway, I began to brace myself for the beating that was surely going to come.

"You can't do this to me," he said quietly.

"What about me? You can't do this to *me!*"

"You're just a whole bunch of surprises this morning, aren't you?" His voice remained quiet and, in a way, that was more menacing than the yelling would have been. "Listen, cunt, you're going to make this movie. You *are* going to do it!"

"I'd rather take the beating."

"We're not talking about any beating," Chuck said. "This is direct disobedience to a fucking order. You know the only choice you've got? You make this movie or you're going to die. That's your big choice."

Chuck led me back into the main room. Wolf and his assistant were sitting behind a small table. Chuck joined them on their side of the table.

"Okay, Linda," Wolf said, "why don't you get undressed and we'll get on with this."

"No."

"I'd advise you to think that over pretty carefully," Wolf said.

"You better think about it," the assistant piped up.

I looked at the three men. And then I noticed that on the small table directly in front of them there was a gun, a revolver. This was a gun I had never seen before, and I assumed that it belonged to either Wolf or his assistant.

"Now are you *sure* you don't want to make this movie?" Wolf said.

"You better be sure," his assistant said.

"Take off your clothes, cunt," Chuck said.

All I could see was the gun—the gun and the odds. They were three to one—three men and one gun against me. As I reached up to unbutton my blouse, I knew I was surrendering. If I could have foreseen how bad it was going to be, I wouldn't have surrendered. I would have chosen the possibility of death. I am able to handle almost everything that has happened to me in my life—even the Holiday Inn gang bang—but I'm still not able to handle that day. A dog. An animal. I've been raped by men who were no better than animals, but this was an actual animal and that represented a huge dividing line.

Wolf had worked out a little story for his movie. When the film began I was to be in bed with Rob who would stay with me for just a few minutes, just long enough to seem to get me aroused, and then leave me. At that point, I was supposed to look frustrated, unsatisfied.

As Wolf directed the action, he said, "Now look around the room. Slowly, slowly. Now you see your dog and you go 'Oooooh!' and now you look excited. Make it look like all of a sudden you're coming up with a brilliant idea. That's right, now snap your fingers."

When Rob completed his part and left, they brought in the animal. I don't know one breed of dog from another.

This was a tan-colored dog with short hair, taller and skinnier than a German Shepherd. The dog's owner, a young man in his mid-twenties, sat down beside the table with the gun.

"You sure this baby knows what to do?" Wolf said.

"Oh, yeah, don't worry about old Norman," he said. "We tried him out last night and you don't have to worry about Norm. He knows the score."

"You tried him out last night?" Wolf said. "You sure that was a smart thing to do?"

"This old fellow can go all day and all night," the owner said. "Don't sweat it. Last night was just to remind him what to do. Him and my old lady got it on last night."

"He got it on with your old lady?" Even Wolf was having difficulty following that one.

"Yeah, and he was fantastic," the young man said. "It's a good thing I'm not the jealous type."

My mind was jumping all over the place. If his old lady was so good with the dog, why didn't they just let her do the movie? Then I looked at the dog and I was afraid of him—more than anything else, I was afraid he was going to bite me. The names of the men suddenly struck me as ironic: *Wolf, as in animal, and Traynor, as in Trainer!* I still couldn't accept what was going to happen.

They put me over on the mattress, turned on the lights and called for the dog. The dog was looking at me beady-eyed, and I had the eerie sensation that he knew more about what was going to happen than I did.

"Okay, Linda, now pet the dog," Wolf said. "That's right, pet the dog. Now get him to lie down."

When I touched the dog, he pulled back. Fortunately, the animal didn't seem interested in human perversions.

"Tell me something," the director asked the owner, "did Norman here let your old lady go down on him?"

"What do you mean?" The young man took offense at that thought. "You think I'd let her do something like that?"

Since the dog did not want to be touched directly, we faked that part of it. Then they had the dog stand upright and put his paws on my shoulders, just like he was giving me a hug. Each time the dog did what was wanted, his owner slipped him a dog biscuit.

"Okay," Wolf said, "now we'll try a little foreplay. Hey, how's your dog with foreplay?"

"Just sensational is all," the owner said.

They had the dog lick me. All that time they were telling me to smile and to laugh. I was supposed to look very excited. I was feeling nothing but acute revulsion. Even as this was happening to me, I had trouble believing it.

I tried thinking something else, anything else, but there was no escaping the dog. How long did this last? How much time was I actually with the dog? Maybe an hour or two but there seemed no end to it. I felt sure he would bite me. I was in a fog of fear.

"Okay, Linda, get down on your hands and knees. No, down on all fours. That's right . . ."

It went on and on, without end, until Wolf's voice came through the fog.

"Okay, we got enough," he said. "Wow, far *out!*"

"I never thought we'd get this," his assistant said.

When they pulled the dog away from me, I was in the deepest valley I'd ever been in, devastated, wanting only to die. I looked up and saw Chuck. The missing finger.

"It's too bad you couldn't bring that other broad," Wolf said. "This fuckin' dog is game for more. Lookit him—we got a real winner here. Hey, nice dog, good dog."

"He could've handled two easy," the dog's owner said.

The men went on that way, talking about the dog and what a winner he was. They sounded as excited as little boys. I suppose they had finally succeeded in doing something they wanted to do for a long time.

Chuck wasn't joining in the talk. He was staring at me, studying me, measuring my reaction. He had to realize this was the worst moment of my life. And he would use it against me forever. From then on if I didn't do something he wanted, he'd bring me a pet, a dog.

Did this give me the strength to kill him or to make a new escape attempt? No. For some reason, it had an opposite effect on me. Every new degradation made me weaker and more docile. Now I felt totally defeated. There were no greater humiliations left for me. The memory of that day and that dog does not fade the way other memories do. The overwhelming sadness that I felt on that day is with me at this moment, stronger than ever.

It was a bad day, such a bad day.

# *ten*

---

Like many other American high-school girls, I worshipped the movie stars. The faces of Clint Eastwood and Elvis and Clark Gable looked down at me from my bedroom walls. There was no way I would miss a Susan Hayward movie. I hungrily read the fan magazine legends and fables. I believed them. I just *knew* that Lana Turner was discovered while sitting on a soda-fountain stool in Hollywood.

My own movie career didn't follow the typical Hollywood patterns. Consider, for example, the way I was discovered. Not at some soda-fountain. I was spotted in one of those miserable eight-millimeter porno epics.

My discoverer was Gerard Damiano, later notorious as the director of *Deep Throat* and *The Devil in Miss Jones*. Damiano had seen me in an eight-millimeter movie and then hired me to be in some of his own. Believe it or not, this was a giant step up. Compared to men like Bob Wolf, Gerry Damiano was Cecil B. De Mille.

Both Wolf and Damiano made porn, but there was a difference. While Wolf worked with one other man, Damiano used a crew of six. Damiano paid Chuck $75.00 for my services, as opposed to the $50.00 that the other eight-millimeter moguls offered. The major difference: I had the feeling that Damiano might actually have film in his camera.

More often than not, people like Wolf began and ended their movies in the same bed. With them there was never such a thing as a change of costume or even, for that matter, a costume. With Damiano the actors began fully clothed and slowly got undressed; they might even move from one room to another. After that, however, they all followed the same basic script. It all came down to the same stuff, but the mood was different. At least no one was urinating on anyone.

Since this was the Christmas season—the Christmas just before my twenty-second birthday—Gerard Damiano was using a holiday backdrop for his movies. They were shot with Christmas trees and Christmas gifts, and there was one scene where we carried Christmas candles. All very sentimental.

My new co-star, Harry Reems, the man who became *the* porn superstar, was a close friend of Damiano's. Before sharing the billing in *Deep Throat,* Harry and I had already done one eight-millimeter together. Harry was playing a very sick man, and I was portraying a nurse in a mini-uniform. Whenever I bent over to give him his medicine, my backside was sticking out. Then when I took the covers away from Harry, his thing was all wrapped up in bandages and gauze. That was the way it began. It ended, of course, with a miracle cure. This short film clip was later inserted, without much logic or explanation, into the middle of *Deep Throat.*

Chuck didn't like Harry Reems at all. I assumed this was because Harry was young and good-looking. When I saw how upset Chuck was, I decided I would pretend to enjoy it with Harry. When Damiano was through filming, Chuck could hardly wait to get me alone.

"What the fuck do you call that?" he snapped.

"What do you mean?"

"Don't try and tell me you weren't really into that," he said. "You were *too* fucking into it, if you ask me."

"I don't know what you're talking about, Chuck." All

innocence. "You're always going around telling me that I'm not freaky enough and that I should get into it more. What do you want from me?"

After that first film, Harry Reems became an ally. Harry has a very good sense of humor—but he was really interested in only one thing, making dirty movies. He was always taking me to one side and telling me that I could make a fortune in porno; he told me that he could arrange a whole lot of eight-millimeter work. All this attention was driving Chuck crazy.

Gerry Damiano became friendly with me and treated me very politely. He was hung up on one thing, the oral-sex techniques that Chuck had taught me, the sword-swallowing or deep-throat trick. He had never known anyone else able to do that.

Then, one day while driving from his apartment to his Manhattan office, Gerry Damiano had an inspiration. Chuck and I were in his office when he arrived and he couldn't wait to tell us his big idea.

"I was driving over the bridge when it hit me," he said. "We're going to do a whole film—and I mean a feature, thirty-five millimeters—about a girl who has her clit in her throat."

He paused to let that sink in. He seemed to be waiting for my reaction. My *reaction?* I was still trying to figure out what he was talking about. A girl with her clit in her throat? Could that have been what he said?

"Hey, that's cool," Chuck said.

"I've even got a title," Damiano said. *"Deep Throat.* It came to me all at once."

That must have been some drive into the city. Not only had Damiano come up with the title and the plot, he had even worked out a theme song, also entitled *Deep Throat.* Thereafter Gerry never stopped humming that melody, and every day he added a verse or two until he came up with the song that was used in the movie. Who could ever forget those lyrics?

*Deep Throat*
*Don't row a boat*
*Don't get your goat*
*That's all she wrote*
*Deep Throat*

"And, Linda," Damiano said, "you're the only girl for this movie."

"You're talking about a feature, right?" Chuck said.

"Thirty-five millimeters," the director said, "and Linda will be perfect for it."

"You're right there," Chuck said. "There's no one else on earth can do it like Linda."

"You know, it's not just that." Damiano turned thoughtful for a moment. "The most amazing thing about Linda, the truly amazing thing, is she still looks sweet and innocent. I don't know how come, but that's one thing I can't buy, sweet innocence."

Damiano's opinions were definitely not shared by his partner, Lou Peraino, the man who put up the money for *Deep Throat*. Another partner in the venture was named Phil Parisi but most of my dealings were with Damiano and Lou Peraino, who was always called Lou Perry in articles and books about the movie. If that's what he wants—I'll call him Lou Perry here.

This was to be Lou's first feature film—pornographic or otherwise—and he wanted a more traditional female star; he kept saying he wanted a blonde with big boobs. But Damiano held out for sweetness and innocence.

"We've never even seen this broad talk," Lou complained.

"So we'll give her a little test," Damiano said. "We'll see if she can talk."

My test for the role struck me as a strange one. Damiano asked me to recite an old nursery-school poem, *Mary Had a Little Lamb*.

"What?" I said.

"You know, 'Mary had a little lamb, Its fleece was white as snow,' and so on."

So that was my screen test for *Deep Throat*. I stood there and recited *Mary Had a Little Lamb* two different ways— first a straight dramatic reading, then laughing all the way through as though it was hilarious. I guess they were testing my dramatic range as well as my voice. It seemed a peculiar selection when compared to the kind of lines I'd be asked to deliver in just a couple of weeks. But I went along with it.

"Linda, the part is yours," Damiano said.

Still, Lou Perry remained unconvinced. As nearly as I could tell, the partnership between Perry and Damiano took the form of a non-stop fight. It seemed to be an equal partnership in that neither of them ever seemed to have the last word. Some of those shouting matches went on all day. As I came to understand their arrangement, Lou Perry was putting up the money and Damiano was doing the work.

When the film started to do extremely well at the box office, Damiano was pressured out of the partnership. I read a story that said he sold his entire share in the film for $25,000. When a reporter asked him why he allowed himself to be bought out so cheaply, Damiano said, "Look, do you want me to get both my legs broken?"

And that says more about Lou Perry than I could ever say. Lou was about forty-five years old, heavy, and sloppy. What I remember most about him was his loud mouth; he was always yelling at someone about something. And he never went anywhere without his bodyguard, Vinnie. Vinnie was some piece of work. He had worked many years for Lou's father, Tony Peraino, and then had been assigned to his son.

Old Tony dropped in to see his son from time to time. He came with his own small army, all wearing dark suits and trenchcoats, looking like they were trying out for an Edward G. Robinson movie. Tony had given his son the $25,000 bankroll for the movie.

That's why it was so important to Lou that the movie be

a success. And it also explains why Lou was so critical of me. It wasn't just that I might ruin his first film or cost him his $25,000. But worse, I might make him look bad in front of daddy.

I will say this about Lou Perry, he never talked behind my back. Anything he had to say about me he said right to my face and generally at the top of his voice. Lou and Damiano were in nearby offices and they constantly shouted their opinions from one room to the next. Lou would point out that this was their first feature film and that their entire futures were riding on it. Damiano would say that he understood that perfectly and that's why they should use me. Lou would shout back that he had never heard of a female star of a pornographic movie without big tits.

"Big tits sell tickets!" he said.

"Linda stays!" Damiano shouted back.

And I did. The director gave me a script, my first movie script. My total speaking part came to about five pages. I looked at the pages but I couldn't bring myself to read them, not right away. They were the first lines I'd ever speak in front of a movie camera, and I had a pretty good idea what kind of lines they'd be. The only thing that remotely interested me was how they'd explain the clitoris in the throat. Chuck was the one who seemed excited by the script; he couldn't understand why I wasn't memorizing my lines that first day.

There was one other thing that excited Chuck. The salary. Chuck was to be paid a flat $100.00 a day for my role in the movie, a total of $1,200. When Lou Perry kept criticizing me, Chuck began to panic that all that money would fall through. One day Chuck came up with a brainstorm.

"We could get Lou to change his mind," he told me, "if you'd just go in there and give him a blow job."

I was familiar with all the Hollywood legends—including some of the casting-couch stories—and I knew that some starlets would take care of movie producers sexually, but that was *before* they got the role, not afterwards.

"The thing is, this guy is really down on you," Chuck said. "He doesn't want you no way, and you've got to fucking convince him that you'll be sensational in the role. I'll go set it up with him. When you go in there, I want you to do a real job on him. I want you to show him you're some kind of a freak. If this doesn't work, your ass is in trouble."

Chuck went into Lou's office and the two men talked for just a couple of minutes. Then Chuck came out for me. My husband signaled for me to go into Lou's office. The two other people in the outer office—Rose the secretary and Vinnie the bodyguard—watched me as I walked over to the door. I could feel their eyes on my back. I felt like a piece of garbage walking through the door—even worse when I came back five minutes later.

Lou's office was a long thin room with a long thin window. I walked in the door. He was seated at his desk, going through piles of paper. He glanced up at me for just a second and then returned to his paperwork.

"Lock the door," he said, not looking at me.

I closed the door behind me and turned the lever that locked the knob. Then I walked over to Lou. He still wasn't looking at me. His eyes remained on those precious piles of paper but he had swiveled his chair so that his legs were no longer under his desk. He had undone his zipper.

"C'm'on," he said. "Let's get this over with."

I went over beside him and got down on my knees and started to work on him. As I was doing what I had to do, he went on fussing with the papers on his desk. Then he suddenly stopped, leaned back in his chair and looked up at the ceiling. His whole body stiffened, relaxed, stiffened again.

"All right," he said. "Get out of here now."

I got to my feet and walked over to the door. I hated what I was going to see on those faces in the outer office. I was garbage. Pure garbage. Then I started getting worried. Had I done it well enough? If I had done it well enough, why did he treat me like such dirt? What would he say to Chuck?

As I walked into the outer office, I felt as though the

secretary was looking at me with contempt. Chuck was staring at my face, looking for some clue. Vinnie, the bodyguard, was the only one with the grace to be looking out the window.

At any rate, I guess it wasn't too disappointing an experience for Lou. Because we went through the same routine every day after that. Exactly the same routine. He always greeted me with, "All right, lock the door." He'd be ready for me and I'd do it. Then I'd hear, "All right, get out of here."

I don't think it ever took him more than three or four minutes. But in that space of time he always managed to let me know that I was no more than garbage. And I'm not sure that all that effort accomplished any change in his attitude. He went right on complaining to Damiano about my physical shortcomings and saying that I was going to send his $25,000 investment down the drain.

Nine months later, after *Deep Throat* had made millions of dollars, Lou became slightly nicer to me. Chuck still made me go into his office, but now Lou's attitude was different. Now, while I was doing it, he would put his hands on my head and pat my hair and then he would say, "Ah, that was good." Unfortunately, I never could stand it when a man put his hands on my head.

This happened, all told, about a dozen times and each time lasted only a few minutes. Why the big rush? He seemed to be worried that his wife would come in unannounced. One day, just as I was starting to work on him, his secretary put a telephone call through. The only call allowed through was a call from his wife. Lou immediately straightened up in his chair and waved me away from him.

"Unh, yeah, I'm kinda busy," he said. "What's on your mind?"

He was trying to carry on a normal conversation with his wife. I don't know how it sounded to her, but to me it was very strained. Later, after hanging up the phone, he was unable to get back in the mood.

After a week of hanging around in New York, Damiano finally told us that they were ready to start filming the movie in Florida. We were to drive down there with Lou's father, Tony Peraino.

I liked old Tony much better than Lou. Tony, then in his sixties, had a dress business in Florida. I got the feeling that there wasn't much that he hadn't seen and done, but I got this feeling not so much from what he said as from what he did not say. He was tall, heavy-set, gray-haired, and always smiling.

Tony did the driving and Chuck did most of the talking. Unsurprisingly, Chuck kept trying to interest the old man in me all the way to Florida. And when we stopped at a motel for the night, Chuck would invent elaborate reasons why I should go to old Tony's room and knock on his door. This was just standard fun-and-games for Chuck but Tony wouldn't go along with it. One morning, as we were beginning our drive south, the old man made his feelings clear on the subject. It was not a case of like son, like father.

"I must be getting old," Tony began. "The way the world is changing, the things young people are doing these days. It's too much for me to understand." For once Chuck was listening, not talking. "You know, they say a lot of things about us Italians but one thing you got to admit, Italian men do not cheat on their wives. Not as a rule, they don't."

Chuck Traynor—his mother was a Traino—was completely quiet now. I had never heard anyone lecture Chuck on anything, and this was beginning to sound very much like a lecture.

"You know why that's so?" the old man went right along, driving as smoothly as he was talking. "I'll tell you why this is so. It's because an Italian man, when he gets a good woman he don't want to lose her. Me, I personally wouldn't take a chance like that, if you follow what I'm saying."

We were both following what he was saying. And he didn't have to say any more than that. Chuck immediately stopped trying to push me on to the old man. I kept thinking of the contrasts between the two Perainos—old Tony stopping Chuck before he could even get started; the son, sitting in his office chair, unzippered, waiting.

I don't think I'm kidding myself about Tony Peraino. I'm not claiming he never did anything wrong. After all, he was supplying the money for making the movie. And he knew what kind of movie it was going to be. But at least he had some values, some code of behavior. If I were to judge by the kind of people I'd been meeting, any values at all qualified a person for the priesthood.

Old Tony reminded me that not everyone in the world was like Chuck. I needed that reminder from time to time. I always had difficulty turning to other people for help; I imagined they'd all turn out like Chuck. Even now, several years after the fact, I get the feeling—and I can be walking down a quiet street in a sleepy village when it hits me—that there is something of Chuck Traynor in everyone.

Back then I had hardly any feelings left. If Chuck told me to go and do something, no matter how unspeakable, I went and did it. Things like that meant less and less to me. I believed without question that there was no alternative, no choice, no escape. I did a great many things with no feeling at all.

So when Chuck told me we were going to make the movie, I knew we were going to make the movie. To me, *Deep Throat* was just another eight-millimeter movie, only longer. I wasn't looking forward to it. It was the next thing to do and it would have to be done.

Chuck was nowhere near as complacent as I was. He saw *Deep Throat* as a big step up, a chance to prove himself. Since we arrived in Miami several days ahead of the rest of the cast, he decided that he was going to coach me for my role in the movie. The movie company put us up at a motel on Biscayne Boulevard, unfortunately a motel with an Olympic-sized swimming pool. I say "unfortunately" because every day Chuck had me out in that swimming pool doing laps for hours at a time. I've never been much of a swimmer, mostly because I tend to fill up with water rather rapidly, but Chuck saw this as a challenge. As I splashed slowly from one end of the pool to the other, Chuck paced along the side of the pool, shouting instructions and criticism, just as though he were training me for the Olympics, not for an appearance in a porno movie.

After our training sessions, Chuck would try to impress upon me the importance of *Deep Throat* to our lives. This was about as close as we ever came to having a conversation.

"We're getting rid of the flab," he said one day. "These people don't want flabby people in their movie."

"Okay."

"What you don't fucking realize is that this is the best thing ever happened to you. Not just the bread. It's—there could be other movies after this one. Bigger movies. This is our big fucking break and you better fucking see that. And this time you better look like you're into it. Just this once would you mind trying?"

"Okay."

"You know something else?" he said. "This is the biggest thing *I've* ever pulled off. Think about it. Where would you be without me? Without me, you'd never have learned a fucking thing. You look at it that way, I'm the one who taught you everything. I'm responsible for all this."

"Yes, Chuck."

# *eleven*

---

When the cast and crew arrived from New York several days later, we all made our headquarters at the Voyager Inn on Biscayne Boulevard. The crew consisted of Norman, the sound man; Juan, the cameraman; Harry, the gaffer, and several others. The "actors" consisted of two men and two women from New York, some others from Florida and, to be sure, Harry Reems.

I continued to get along with Harry just fine. One reason Harry Reems became a porn superstar—I suppose *the* male superstar of pornographic movies—is that he appears to be fairly intelligent and he has a good sense of humor. Harry's strongest appeal to me, however, was the fact that Chuck did not like him at all.

Chuck constantly referred to Harry Reems as "that asshole," and Harry pretended that Chuck did not exist. Every time Harry had a chance to speak with me alone, he'd tell me he could make me a star, that I should join him in making bigger and better porno movies. The implication was always there: Harry would take care of everything once I got myself away from you-know-who.

In the days before the actual shooting, I worked harder

127

than I ever had before in my life. Whenever Chuck let me stop swimming, he had me memorizing the script. Memorizing my lines was not a particularly difficult feat. The movie opened with my looking for my girlfriend. I think my first line was about as complicated as, "Helen?" In *Deep Throat* the lines were strictly secondary to the action; what made the movie successful was not what was said, but what we did.

That first day of shooting, everyone was in a good mood. Director Gerry Damiano was happy to be away from his shouting matches with Lou Perry. He spent much of each day constructing new verses for the *Deep Throat* theme song, and he was so light-hearted and full of energy that his mood became contagious.

For the first time in many months I began to feel better. It had been a cold and dreary January in New York, but it was warm in Florida. Now, with the movie being shot, Chuck wasn't able to get me involved in any of his other ventures or adventures. Sure, I was still his personal prisoner, but I was only going to have to fuck one person, Harry Reems.

I use that word—"fuck"—because it fit the act. What I was doing then had nothing whatsoever to do with making love. In my mind there is a world of difference between fucking and making love. I think that "fuck" is an extremely ugly word and with that in mind, I use it here.

At the beginning of the movie there was none of that at all. In fact, the first day we set up the outside shots, what they called the "exteriors," around the motel swimming pool. The mood of the previous few days carried into the actual shooting. The crew members were all in high spirits, telling jokes, playing pranks, goofing on the director and, somehow, despite all this, taking some pictures.

Something was happening to me, something strange. It had to do with the fact that no one was treating me like garbage. And maybe it was just the chemistry of being part of a group. For the first time in many months, I was thrown in with other people, other people who weren't perverted and threatening. I became *part* of a group. I began to ease up.

The first scene called for me to be sitting beside the pool in a bathing suit while an actor dove into the pool, swam across it, and splashed some water on me. One of the crew members did something funny—I can no longer remember what—but everyone started laughing, and I was laughing along with the rest of them.

*I was laughing along with the rest of them.* And I thought my face would break. I hadn't laughed, really laughed, in so long that my face had to carve new smile lines. That thought struck me as funny, and I laughed some more; then I just let it all come out.

We laughed a lot that first day of shooting while we were doing the poolside shots, the walking-down-the-street shots and the knocking-on-the-door shots. And no one was asking me to do anything I didn't want to do.

That night, back in the motel room, I was still feeling fine. The entire crew was in the very next room having a party. They were drinking, smoking pot, carrying on—and the sounds of partying came clearly into our room. There was only one person who was not having a good time. Chuck. Throughout the day he had gotten more and more sullen; now he was staring across the room at me with low-burning hatred.

I had to get away from him and that intensity. I went into the bathroom, removed my makeup, and took a shower. When I went back out into the bedroom, nothing had changed. The party in the next room was still going full blast, and Chuck's expression was the same.

"What's the matter now?" I asked.

"You cunt!"

"What *is* the matter?"

"Your smile!" he said. "That fucking smile of yours. You were so busy smiling all day—well, let's see you smile now. Why don't you smile for me now?"

"What do you want from me? What're you talking about?"

"I'm talking about your fucking smile. You walk around smiling all day like some idiot Mona Lisa. Smiling at the crew. Smiling at Damiano. Smiling at that asshole Reems."

"You told me I should look like I was into it."

"I didn't tell you to go around *smiling!*" Chuck was yelling at me now, and I realized that the party sounds from the next room had stopped. "You don't have to smile like some idiot. And *laughing!* What was that all about? I didn't see anything to laugh about. Why was everyone laughing around the pool?"

"It was just something funny."

*"It was just something funny."* Chuck loved to mimic me. *"What* was so funny? I didn't see anything that was funny. You think this is funny now? You cunt, you think there's something funny going on now?"

"What're you talking about?" Suddenly I was screaming back at him, angry, too. Oh, that was some day, the first time in many months that I had been able to feel laughter *and* anger. Just feeling anything again felt good. Even the anger felt good and I let it all out.

"First you yell at me because I look too sad, and now you yell at me because I'm smiling too much! *Smiling too much!* You ought to see a doctor, Chuck, you really ought to. Because you're crazy."

"I'm not the one who is going to need a doctor."

I was going to be in for it now. Talking back to Chuck was a major offense. My only hope was the men in the next room. It had grown as quiet as a tomb in there; they had to be hearing everything that was being said. For the first time, help seemed at hand.

"And I know why you're so mad," I said.

"Shut up!"

"You're mad because it's like you're losing some of your power."

"Cunt!"

The first punch sent me crashing over backwards onto the

bed. The minute I had said that about his losing power, I realized it was the truth. He knew it was true, too. The presence of other people diminished him and diluted my fear of him. It gave me courage.

And this is what made him go insane. Most often when Chuck beat me, it was in the manner of someone training an animal—cold-blooded and methodical and to make a point. Not this time. He went berserk. He picked me up off the bed and threw me against the wall separating us from the crew.

"Stop!" I was screaming as a way of getting the attention of the men in the next room. "Please stop! You're hurting me!"

He tore my bathrobe off in two pieces. I wriggled away from him and went down to the floor. By this time I had learned that the best way to handle a beating was to roll myself up into a tight ball on the floor—protecting my breasts and my stomach from his boots. When I was curled up that way, most of his kicks hit me on the legs.

This happened enough so that today my legs are still a mess. Not too long ago, I went to see a doctor in New York about having the surface veins removed from my legs and he couldn't believe what he was seeing. He said, "My God, what happened to you?"

Well, this was what happened to me. This beating and many others like it.

"Help!" I called out. "Oh, God, please help me! *Someone,* help me!"

Help did not come. Chuck was still in a frenzy, kicking hard at me with his boots while I squeezed myself into a tighter and tighter ball. I held my breath, waiting for the men in the next room to build up their courage and come to my aid. I *knew* they would. They knew I was in trouble. In the past I had always been surrounded by strangers, and I didn't expect that a stranger would help. But these men were not strangers. We had just spent a long day together.

We had kidded with each other, laughed at the same jokes, behaved the way friends behave with each other. Where were they? Why didn't they come?

Before then I wouldn't have yelled at Chuck and I wouldn't have screamed for help. That would always mean a worse beating for me. But on this day, I was willing to take that chance. But no one came. The beating went on until Chuck finally got physically tired and stopped.

After the beating, I lay curled on the floor while Chuck turned on the television set. I wanted to get up and go back into the hot shower, but I knew I'd have to ask permission first. And I wasn't up to that. As I lay there on the floor, Chuck was walking around, whistling, feeling chipper, back in control. Finally, I surrendered.

"Chuck, can I go to bed now?"

"Yeah," he said. "Why not?"

I dragged myself over to the bed and fell into it. Chuck was watching a war movie. There were still no sounds from the next room. I guess my screaming must've ruined their party. There were at least a half-dozen of them. They could have handled Chuck. But no. No one did anything until the next day. And then what they did was to try to conceal my bruises.

The next morning, I went into the motel cafeteria for breakfast. I was wearing shorts and large bruise marks had already formed on my legs. Chuck was making a phone call when Gerry Damiano came over to speak to me. His eyes went right to my legs.

"Oh, for crying out loud!" he said. "What's that all about?"

"What?"

"Those bruises all over your legs, what're they all about?"

"They're just bruises. I can't talk about them."

"Well, I can," he said. "Those bruises happen to be very important to me. We'll do what we can to cover them up, but they'll show up in the movie. I mean, one reason you got this job—believe it or not, Linda, this is the *main* reason —is that you looked so fresh and young. So innocent. How innocent are you going to look with those marks all over your body?"

"I couldn't do anything about it."

"But what brought it about? I wouldn't have guessed that Chuck was going to turn into the jealous type."

"That's not it. It's not because he's jealous."

"Well, we better be sure about that," Damiano said. "If he is jealous, what's he going to be like later on when the scenes are coming down between you and Harry?"

"I don't think he'll do anything else," I said. "He doesn't care what anyone else does to me. I think the reason he beat me up was I was having too good a time. He says I was smiling too much."

"I'm not sure I follow that."

"If you ever figure it out, explain it to me."

When I got to the set, I could feel the difference in mood. No more jokes. No one seemed able to look me in the eyes. One of the other girls on the set had makeup with her and together we painted over the bruises. But the camouflage was not perfect. If you saw the movie, you must have seen the huge black-and-blue marks on my thighs and legs.

Later that morning Damiano sent us out to buy a nurse's uniform. As the director was giving Chuck the instructions, I was joined by Norman, the sound man. Norman was quiet and shy and always seemed to be hiding out behind his sunglasses. He started speaking to me out of the side of his mouth, rapidly, his eyes on Chuck all the time.

"Look, Linda, we had no idea how bad it is."

"You didn't?"

"If you need help, just let me know. I mean, if there's anything any of us can do, just give us a signal."

"What can anyone do?"

"I don't know," he said. "We could help." He sped up the talk as he saw Chuck and Damiano winding up their conversation. "I mean it, just let us know. We heard what was going on last night. And I just want you to know I'm here."

I could see that much. He was here. I didn't say a word but I know what I was thinking: sure, you're here now but where were you last night? Where were you when you were needed? Where was anyone? It was nice, and it may have been brave of him to offer help, but it was too late; the corpse was being thrown a lifesaver. It was an offer that couldn't be accepted, because it was an offer that couldn't be trusted. He was just saying words with nothing behind them.

Does that sound too hard? Maybe so. But I am tough on people. Most people don't know how hard I judge them because I don't say anything. All I do is cross them off the list. Forever. These men had their chance to help me and they didn't respond. If someone is your friend—really your friend—they don't let a chance like that pass by. When someone needs help, that's the time to help. Not the next day. Not when it's safe.

And so I stopped smiling. And now, whenever we shot a scene, I would hear, "Smile, Linda" and "Please smile, Linda" and "Just try one little smile, Linda." But those smiles were harder and harder to come by. If I smiled too much, Chuck would beat me. And now I knew that no one would lift a finger to help me. The guys on the set tried to cheer me up by goofing around, but there was no longer anything to smile about.

We started doing the interior shots, many of them in homes borrowed for the movie. Now that I was completely sobered up, I could see how absurd my role in the movie was. In the movie I play some weird kind of visiting nurse. My job was to go around and make people feel better. Mostly men, needless to say.

The big scene in the movie is when Harry Reems, playing a doctor, discovers that my clitoris has been misplaced and is located in my throat. Although we tried this scene several times, we could never get it quite right. We never had any trouble with the action, only with the lines. We'd do the sex scenes just once and then we'd hear Damiano say, "That's a take!" But when we so-called actors had a simple line or two to deliver, we'd be there for hours trying to get it right. One scene went on until four in the morning. We couldn't figure out why one of the actresses was having such trouble with her lines until Damiano discovered that she had never learned to read.

Harry and I took turns messing up our lines in one big scene until Damiano finally lost his patience. Then the director took the unprecedented step of calling for a rehearsal. Harry and I were told to keep going over the lines until we got them right.

"It's not so bad," Harry was supposed to say, "You should be thankful you have a clitoris at all."

"That's easy for you to say," I replied through teardrops. "How would you feel if your balls were in your ear?"

"Why then I could hear myself coming!" Harry said.

Well, on this day it was hard not to laugh. As we went over the idiotic lines time and time again, they seemed funnier and funnier. Everytime I lamented my missing clitoris —"I want to hear bells ringing, dams bursting, and rockets exploding"—we'd break up. Harry would say something like, "Tell me, Linda, exactly why is that you want to hear a dam burst?" and that would be enough to set us off.

Damiano joined our little rehearsal as Harry was examining the spot where the clitoris is normally located, and he kept finding other objects: A golden pocket watch . . . things like that. And every time he found a strange object, he would say. "Oh, my God, what have we here?"

The three of us were all laughing at that when suddenly, without anyone saying a word, we stopped and swiveled around toward Chuck who was staring at us from the other side of the large dimly lit room. His eyes seemed to burn through the darkness. The laughing died and we all froze for a long moment before returning to the scene. Chuck decided we had rehearsed the scene enough.

"I don't see why they have to go over that again," he said. "They've got the lines down now."

"Let them be," Damiano said. "I want them to get them cold."

"Yeah, well how many times do they have to go over the same stuff?"

"Chuck, do me a little favor, will you?" Damiano said. "Would you go out and pick up the sandwiches? We're about to break for lunch."

Chuck was grumbling as he went out for the food, but he did go. And from that moment on, Chuck became Damiano's gofer—he'd go for coffee, beer, lunch, cigarettes, practically anything that would keep him out of the way. Once Chuck was gone, Damiano would close the set so that he couldn't return until we completed shooting the scene. This was his way of keeping Chuck and Harry Reems apart.

"You see the way they're treating me?" Chuck would complain in private. "They don't seem to realize that I'm the man who trained the star. I mean, who was it brought you to New York in the first place? If it wasn't for me, they wouldn't have a fucking star, and they wouldn't have this fucking movie. And here they are, treating me like some damn errand boy."

It still hadn't dawned on me that this was going to be a big movie that would someday be shown in a theater on a real movie screen. *Deep Throat* would be important to me in many ways, but I didn't realize that then. To me it would be at once a low point and a salvation.

As it was happening, it seemed insignificant. The film itself only took up twelve days of my life—six before the cameras, another six waiting around for the sun to come out. Probably the most important thing to happen to me was a rechristening. Damiano came up with the name Linda Lovelace for the character in his movie. There had been a BB and an MM and now he wanted an LL. In time, I came to dislike the name, Linda Lovelace, because of what it stood for. But the truth is this: Linda Boreman and Linda Traynor never managed to get away from Chuck; it took a Linda Lovelace to escape.

*Deep Throat* seemed just another small chapter of my life, but I hated to see it end. Maybe nothing had really changed, not yet, and maybe I had to be involved sexually with an actor or two, but it was much better than it might otherwise have been. Two weeks of making a movie, even a pornographic movie, was better than two weeks of being a hooker. And being with other people, just listening to others talk, that was nice.

Whenever Chuck was out of sight, one or another of the crew would come up and talk with me. They all said that I could make a fortune in porno movies. If I just had the right manager. And, as luck would have it, each of them had a scam: a script, a producer with money, a pet film project. It always came down to the same thing, "Baby, I can make you a star." Maybe some people would find that flattering, but a career in dirty movies was not something that meant anything to me. Not then, not ever.

Every evening, after we finished shooting for the day, Chuck and I drove the film out to the airport. It was shipped up to Lou in New York where it was processed and studied. And every day Lou would call Damiano to complain. We could only hear Damiano's side of the conversation—so I would hear him yell that I was *not* too skinny, and I was *not* too flat-chested, and I was *not* too amateurish.

Damiano seemed pleased by my work. When we managed a scene in a single take, especially if it was a difficult sexual scene, he would lead the crew in applause. I always found that embarrassing. When things were going smoothly, Damiano liked to pretend that he was a regular movie director. He would say things like, "Lights, camera, action!" And, "Cut!" And, "That's a take." And, one day, "That's a wrap."

None of this fooled me. I never once thought of *Deep Throat* as a regular movie. Not a movie-movie. I'd spent my life watching actresses like Susan Hayward and Claudette Colbert and Bette Davis, and I knew these women would not be caught dead, or even half-dead, in something like *Deep Throat*. Maybe that's why I never felt like an actress, not even with the hot lights on and the cameras grinding.

Similarly, it was impossible to think of Harry Reems as a movie star. My idea of a real movie star was Clark Gable. I would settle for a Dustin Hoffman or an Al Pacino—they're adorable. But Harry Reems?

Harry, like the others who do porn for a living, took himself and his job very seriously. To him, it was his livelihood. On a good week he would take home $700 in tax-free income. My feeling was simple: If someone could be involved in public sex, there was something seriously wrong with him. There were just too many questions. If he could do that much, how could you be sure he wasn't as far-out as Chuck? As far as I could see there was only one difference between Harry and Chuck; Harry was in it for the money and Chuck was in it for weird thrills. But they were both in it.

And that was enough for me. Sometimes I feel that I'm a real prude, more of a prude than anyone I know. Whenever I hear someone talking about the sexual revolution or the new sexual freedom, I don't look on that as progress. People who are into promiscuity—I'm sorry to say—have a problem. My feeling is this: If people can keep it between themselves and their mates, that's just fine. But love-making should be a two-person proposition. No more, no less. It's just nobody else's business.

# *twelve*

---

*Deep Throat*—such a small slice of my life with Chuck—
two weeks out of more than two years. It would be months
before the film would open, more months before anyone
would hear about it, still more months before the name Linda
Lovelace would become known throughout the world.

On the way to Jersey City to pick up our belongings,
we were not alone. We had a hitchhiker with us, a sixteen-
year-old runaway named Ginger. Chuck was always picking
up female hitchhikers. In fact, that's how he did most of his
recruiting. I was amazed by the way Chuck would pick up
a hitchhiker and ask right off, "Would you like to be a
hooker?" I was even more amazed by the number of young
girls who didn't say no. Ginger was one who didn't say no.

Ginger told us that she had left home because her father
wouldn't keep his hands to himself and her mother wouldn't
believe that story. Ginger was a tiny girl with long blonde
hair, not at all pretty. Though she was only sixteen, life
had toughened her face so that she would never seem sweet
again. She had spent the last year on the road, crisscrossing
the country and living off truck drivers. There was only one
small matter separating her from being a hooker. Money.

"You're doing that shit anyway," Chuck said. "You might as well get paid for it."

"Might as well," she said.

Just before we started out trip north, Chuck fixed Ginger up with her first trick and let her keep the money. Afterwards, she sat on the edge of her bed, staring at two twenty-dollar bills, asking herself the age-old question: "How long has this been going on?"

Life continued as it had before my debut as a movie star, but with a difference. All that exposure to moviemaking had given Chuck a new ambition. Never again would he be someone else's gofer; now he wanted to make his own movies.

On our first day back in the New York area, Chuck borrowed an eight-millimeter camera from Lou Perry. Then he made two movies starring Linda Lovelace and Ginger. One movie was called *The Foot* and the other one was *The Fist*. In addition to coming up with the original concept, the script, and the direction, Chuck also provided the camerawork. It was definitely a Chuck Traynor Production.

*The Foot* opens with a closeup shot of two feet, Ginger's feet. They are seen walking down a city street. Then up a flight of stairs. Then into a bedroom where they are filmed beside two new feet, the feet belonging to a hooker, my feet. Chuck gave us a running explanation of the story as he ran the camera.

"Okay, get ready, here comes the foot," he said. "The foot's gonna give you twenty dollars. Let's see that twenty dollars. Okay. Now you shake your head no, you're telling the foot that's not enough. Okay, so now the foot is giving you ten dollars more. You take the ten and nod your head yes. That's right, that's good. Okay, now the foot is gonna work its way up your leg—that's right, let's see a little toe action—the foot is coming up your leg now and getting you all excited. And now the foot is going to fuck you."

Does all that sound like a joke? I wish it had been a joke. But that's actually the movie that Chuck dreamed up and made. And when he made *The Fist*, he didn't bother to change the plot line at all.

The following day, Chuck returned the cameras and the films to Lou. He was paid $100 for each movie, enough to finance our return trip to Florida. During our last night in Jersey City, Chuck decided he was in the mood for some fun and games. Ginger had dozed off but was not yet in a sound sleep. Chuck took my left hand and placed it on Ginger's breast.

"Whoa right there!" She was wide awake in an instant, sitting up in bed and glaring at Chuck. "What the fuck do you think you're doing? What's this supposed to mean? You think I'm supposed to give you some free entertainment? Jesus Christ, stop being such a creep and let me get some sleep."

Thank God it was dark. Chuck couldn't see my smile. I didn't like Ginger at all—I mean, she may have been the *un*sweetest girl in history—but I certainly did respect her. That night, lying there in bed, I stayed awake, wondering what would have happened if I had been the way Ginger is, if I had been that tough with Chuck from the beginning.

The next morning we began our drive south. We drove as far as North Carolina where we stopped to visit Chuck's mother. When I heard we were going to stay with her for a couple of days, I was wondering whether she would be any help in getting her son off my back.

It didn't take me long to realize that she wouldn't be my ally. Chuck was the apple of her eye; he could do no wrong. Chuck's mother was fiftyish, black-haired, and heavily made up: She favored pale blue eye shadow and black drawn-on eyebrows. She told us stories going back to the time when Chuck was a little boy and she had left his father. She said that at that time she had been friends with some of that era's most notorious mobsters. She called herself a "flower lady" and explained that she had had a florist shop that was used as a front. Although she had been the special friend of one man in particular, she had escorted others as well. And, in fact, she had been too busy to bring up Chuck herself so her parents had adopted him. He had been raised by his grandparents.

I wondered whether this didn't explain a lot about Chuck's attitude toward women. I'm no shrink but it was obvious that he hated women. Did it all begin as a deep resentment toward his mother and the way she was living her life? Maybe the brutality he directed toward me was something he would rather have directed toward his mother. All the time he was forcing me to do perverted and weird things, all those unnatural acts, was he just evening an old score against his mother?

Of course, none of this was visible. When he was with his mother, Chuck became the perfect gentleman. As long as we were under her roof, he was even polite to me. His mother was obviously crazy about her son. She was proud of his having been a Marine, a pilot, and a man in business for himself. She would just ignore it when she learned something less than perfect about her Chucky-poo.

So, for the couple of days that Chuck played the role of good son, I just relaxed, Ginger, however, was getting restless, anxious to get back to Florida. One morning, Chuck dragged us out to wash the car. Chuck went outside and watched us work for a while. But Chuck, the World's Greatest Expert on Practically Everything, could never watch anyone do anything without offering advice. He decided to give Ginger the full benefit of his car-washing experience.

"Hey, that's no way to do that," he said. "You shouldn't be doing those short, straight strokes."

"Get off my case, willya?"

"I'm serious," Chuck said. "When you wash a car, you should make like small circles."

"Really?" Ginger dropped the sponge on the driveway. "Well, fuck you!"

Before walking away, she took the bucket of soapy water and splashed it over the car. She walked into the house. And when she came back out, she was carrying her jacket and her suitcase. She was followed by Chuck's mother who was frantic.

"Your little friend is leaving," Chuck's mother said. "That poor little girl—what's going to happen to her if she's picked up by some tough guys."

"Well, they'll learn what tough is," Chuck said. "Nothing's ever going to happen to that chick that she can't handle. Take it from me, that's one little girl knows just what to do."

Yes, she did! That was the last we saw of Ginger and I couldn't help being envious of her. I don't know what life has offered her since that day in North Carolina—probably not much—but if she's reading these words, I'd like to tell her she did the right thing.

Thoughts of Ginger and her casual "fuck-you" farewell ate at me all the way to Florida. There she was, still a kid, no bigger than a splinter, and she was able to just walk away. Why couldn't I? For almost two years I had been Chuck Traynor's prisoner.

And in that time I had changed: no longer did Chuck have to stand guard over me every minute of the day. Maybe I wasn't exactly a prisoner anymore; maybe I had become a trustee. I was breathing and sleeping and eating but I was no more alive than a zombie. The encounter with Ginger seemed to wake me up, and once again I began to think about escape.

It was the summer of '72 and Chuck and I were back at square one, in Miami, with me working as a hooker and his staring at me through a peephole in the wall. Once again he was trusting me enough so that I could take outside jobs in hotels and apartments.

And why shouldn't he trust me? I was causing him no trouble. After a year of working as a hooker, I still refused to look at myself as a hooker. It was, after all, survival, my only means of staying alive. And that's how I accepted it: as life, but not livelihood. And only very gradually did it become an occupation. It was always degrading and dirty but, in time, it lost much of its terror. I was a hooker the way someone else might be a cashier in a supermarket or a laborer on an assemblyline; not enjoying any of it, but doing it to stay alive. My body did the work, not my mind and heart. If I was a hooker in fact, I was never a hooker in spirit. I was doing it but I was not into it. Looking back now, I feel that it was some other person—that was not me.

Prostitution, like any other occupation, becomes a matter of routines and rituals. There was always a bad moment or two at the beginning—a hooker can never know what lies on the other side of a closed door—but there was a steadily diminishing sense of horror about the rest of it.

It's hard for me to look back and think of myself as a hooker. But if you sort letters for a year-and-a-half in the post office, then you're a mailman. You do it, and you do it, and you do it; then you become it.

Always I was sustained by the hope that this life would be temporary. It could not possibly go on forever. One day it would be all over. But that day seemed no nearer.

Just as I could never accept the thought of myself as a hooker, I never looked at myself as Mrs. Charles Traynor. That, too, was unreal. Chuck would talk about us as being married—he was my "old man" and I was his "old lady"— but that meant nothing to me. If you ever heard him talk about marriage, you'd have to wonder what kind of woman would want to be his wife.

"A woman is supposed to do everything for her husband," Chuck once told me. "Everything. That's the whole setup. If I'm ever sent to prison, you will do everything to get me out of jail. I would expect you to fuck everyone and everything to help me. That's what a wife does."

So I was back then, living up to Chuck's concept of perfect womanhood, fucking everyone and everything to help her husband. But he began to relax his vigilance, and I began to look for ways out once again.

During one of my outside jobs, I had a few minutes alone with a telephone. I called my old friend, Betsy, and asked her to help me get away from Chuck. She said she'd do whatever I wanted. I told her that I was going to be doing a trick at a new Howard Johnson's motel the following night at eight and there might be a way to escape then. Betsy said she'd be waiting in a car in front of the motel.

I had trouble getting to sleep that night, and the next morning I was all jitters. Chuck noticed that my behavior wasn't normal.

"We're going to cancel tonight," he said. "You look like hell."

"Good," I said. "I need the rest."

Chuck's decision to cancel an appointment was not at all unusual. Quite often he cancelled at the last minute. I think this was just another way to keep me off balance. And although I died a little inside when he decided to cancel, I played it cool.

"Since I'm not going out tonight, I think I'll wash my hair."

"Just a damn minute," he said. "Let me think about this."

I can guess what he was thinking about. He was thinking about giving up a $45.00 trick. If it had only been a $25.00 trick, I would have spent the day shampooing my hair.

"Forget it," he said. "We're going."

The rest of the day I concentrated on doing nothing out of the ordinary, nothing that would arouse new suspicions. I wondered if he could hear my racing heart. That night, just before eight o'clock, we pulled up in front of the entrance to the Howard Johnson's. Chuck left the car there, its motor running, and went with me into the lobby. He watched me walk over and go into a waiting elevator. I pushed the button to the correct floor, rode up, stepped off.

Timing would be everything. I imagined Chuck watching the elevator indicator lights, waiting a few minutes and then going out to park his car in the huge parking lot before returning to the lobby where he would wait for me. As the elevator was summoned elsewhere, I waited in the hallway. And then I pushed the button, stepped aboard and took the elevator down to the lobby.

The elevator doors opened and I hesitated a second before stepping out. Standing at the back of the empty car, I looked out to see whether Chuck was in the lobby. It seemed empty. I had just a couple of minutes, and I moved quickly out of the elevator and out of the building and around to the other side.

A car was there, its parking lights turned on. Betsy was there with a young man named Don whom she had been living with. No sooner was I in the car than he pulled away. And as we drove to their house, I told them the story. Everything.

"I was guessing something like that," Betsy said. "I saw one of those movies you made up in New York, the one with the dog. I told Don that you weren't like that, that that wasn't something you'd ever do willingly."

"I guess you were right about that," Don said.

"We tried to find out more," Betsy said. "We went out to the country club where your mother is working. We told her that we thought something was wrong and that you needed some help."

As we drove toward their home, I was in terrible emotional turmoil. Later Betsy told me I acted as though I was drugged and that it took several days before I responded to things in a normal way. Maybe that was just the fear hanging on. I felt no happiness and no relief. Not yet. At nine o'clock Chuck would go upstairs to get me. I imagined the scene, the trick explaining to Chuck that I had never shown. What would happen next?

"You can count on us for anything," Betsy said. "For any help you need. You'll never have to go back to Chuck again."

"I've learned one thing," I said. "Chuck's not going to let me get away this easily."

Betsy's house inspired no confidence. They lived an hour outside Miami in a lower middle-class development, small connected homes with tiny yards. She and Don had rented their home from the leader of a local motorcycle gang. The furnishings reflected the kind of taste I was anxious to escape.

The bedroom had mirrored ceilings, a waterbed, a framed photograph of Betsy wearing a "Merry Widow" corset. When I saw the movie projector stationed beside the bed, I couldn't help but think that Betsy and Don had probably been watching me while they were in bed together. It made me very uneasy.

It's odd but looking back on this escape, it seems to me that it all took place within a day or two. But Betsy tells me that I was with her, away from Chuck, for nearly a week. She also tells me that when Chuck figured out where I was, he called every few hours. At first he was polite and even contrite. He told her that we had a "misuderstanding" and that we just had to talk things out.

I didn't speak to Chuck myself for several days. During those days, according to Betsy, I behaved like someone coming out of a deep sleep. She said that at first she was concerned that something had happened to my brain, but that I was my old self by the end of the week. She said she knew that I was going to be all right when I started cleaning the house for them and scrubbing the floors. Nothing makes me happier than cleaning a house.

I told Betsy that I would speak to Chuck the next time he called. When the phone rang, she was reluctant to give me the receiver.

"It's Chuck," she said, "and he does want to talk with you. But, Linda, you don't have to talk with him at all if you don't want to. I mean that."

I knew I would have to talk with Chuck eventually anyway. However, I was totally unprepared for what I heard.

"Linda, I love you and I need you," Chuck said.

"What?"

"Linda, you are my wife and I'm your husband. We are fucking married! And there is no way we should be apart. Now I know things have not been fucking perfect for you— I can admit that. But there is no way that I'm going to take this shit from you. Now you just make your little goodbyes there and get yourself packed up because I am coming over to get you and that is that!"

"I'm not coming back, Chuck."

It was amazing how much effort that one line took. Chuck filled my heart with terror. Even when he was trying to sweet-talk me—believe it or not, that was sweet talk—he generated nothing but fear.

"You are my old lady," he said, "and we got us a piece of paper that says we will not split until death do us part. Now all I'm saying is for us to get back together. If you got some fucking complaints, we can work these things out. We can fucking *talk* about them. But first we got to get our shit together."

"No, Chuck."

"No? *No!* What is this no? Is this a word a wife uses to a husband?"

I hung up the phone then.

Chuck made one other attempt to be "reasonable." He delivered a letter to the house, and in that letter he promised to mend his ways; he would put up new drapes at home and take care of "all the other little things" that had been bothering me. And then the sweet talk, such as it was, came to an end. It ended officially with another phone call.

"Did you get my letter?"

"Yes."

"Okay, then listen to me, Babe. I want you to knock off this shit right now."

"No."

"*No!* Don't you ever fucking use that word to me again, cunt. Maybe you better know something—there's a van parked outside that house right now."

"What do I care?"

"Well, you better fucking care. You better fucking well care. Why don't you just take yourself a little walk to the window there. Take a good long look at that van parked out there."

I did. And I recognized the van at once. It belonged to

a good friend of Chuck's, the fireman who had testified at
his trial that they were going to start a sky-diving club. I
went back to the phone.

"Did you see the van outside?"

"I saw the van."

"Good," he said. "Now if you think I'm going to let you
just walk out on me, you're fucking crazy. I will kill you
first, and I do believe you know that by now. I will kill you
and every fucking person in that house. That Betsy goes
first; and I will blow her fucking brains all over the wall."

"Chuck, I'm staying here."

"Good, you do that. That's real good. Because I'm on my
way over there, cunt. If you try to leave, you are dead. You
are all dead people. That van has got a machine gun and
enough grenades to blow up that whole fucking shantytown.
If there's any trouble at all—I mean that, any trouble at all
—you are going to be bombed right out of there. Bobby is
out there in the van now. He's got two guys with him and
they've got their fucking orders. They see anything funny,
they blow that place sky high. Don't try to leave."

"I'm not going with you, Chuck."

"The fuck you're not! Listen good, Linda. I'm your old
man and I'm walking up to the front door and I'm coming
into the house and I'm getting you. If I go back out that
door without you, they'll be able to see the blast as far away
as Havana."

I put the phone down.

"Betsy, I'm going to go with him when he comes."

"You don't have to go anywhere."

"I've got to go with him!"

"Did he tell you he was going to blow up the house?"

"Yes."

"Don't let that scare you," Betsy said. "He's been telling
me that all week. When he first started to call, he was very
polite. Then he started in with the threats. I don't even
listen to him any more."

"He means it," I said. "I've seen his machine gun and his

hand grenades. He's not afraid to use them. There's only one way I can think of stopping him, and that's to call the police."

"Yeah, but that's the one thing we can't do," Don said. "The fuzz would love to get in here and rip this place up."

There were many reasons they couldn't allow the police there. Some of the reasons: marijuana, mescaline, LSD, cocaine and a small library of pornographic movies. The police were out of the question.

During the next half hour, the van didn't budge. Betsy, looking out the window at it, saw two rifles in a window. All avenues of thought came to the same dead end; I was already defeated. Betsy tried to reassure me. She told me that they were willing to take their chances with Chuck, and that I really didn't have to go back with him.

When Chuck showed up at the front door, I was in the bathroom. I heard him explaining to Betsy and Don that everything would be all right, that we had just had a little lovers' spat and that he was there to take his old lady back home where she belonged.

"Everything's all right now," he said as I walked into the room. "We can go now, Babe. I think we've bothered these nice people long enough."

His voice was calm but I could sense the tension beneath it. As he spoke to me, he was rubbing one hand against the other, massaging his fingers, tugging at the stump of the missing finger on his right hand. His eyes were somewhere off in the distance, looking at a wall as he said his piece.

"Did you get your clothes?" Chuck was asking. "Why don't you get your things together and we can go tell Bob that he can go home now."

His eyes came down from the wall and focused on Betsy. A look of hatred. He knew that she was my friend and always would be. As long as I had a friend, that meant Chuck didn't own me outright.

"I'll get my things," I said.

As I went into the bedroom, Betsy followed. She closed the door.

"Linda, this is the last time I'm going to be able to say this. If you want a place to stay, you can stay here. I'll take my chances with Chuck."

"He'll kill you."

I left with Chuck then. He said not a word. He was boiling, so angry that he was actually unable to yell. I had hit him where it hurt the most; I had revealed his evilness to other people. Others now knew that he was a sadistic madman. And as we drove off, followed by the ominous red van, I realized where I had been making my mistake.

Each time I tried to escape, I had drawn other people into my plan. Each time my plan failed because of the other people. There was the hooker who called out for Chuck at the last moment; my parents who never understood the danger; and my closest friend who would have been killed. I was resolved that this would not be my last escape attempt; it would only be my last *unsuccessful* escape attempt.

# *thirteen*

---

I knew there would be a punishment, but I had no idea what form that punishment would take. All I knew for sure was that it would be severe. While I was waiting for that, life went back to normal. Which is to say back to what Chuck thought of as normal. Which is also to say back to what the rest of the world would think of as perverted and weird. I was back in a small room having sex with strangers while Chuck was watching me through a peephole.

When he wasn't staring at me through a hole in the wall, Chuck was thinking up strange things for me to do.

What kind of strange things?

You name it. Almost every day, Chuck would tell me to put on a skirt but no underwear. Then we would go into a fast-food joint for something to eat. He would sit me just so and make sure my skirt was hiked up around my hips. Then he would push my legs apart so that I'd be exposed to the other men in the restaurant. His whole kick was watching them react.

And, at least once a day, he would make me take off my sweater while we were driving. Generally that would be as we were driving by an army truck or a busload of ballplayers.

It was all sick but there was no way I could fight it. No way to say no. And exposing myself in public was a lot better than some of his other pranks. For example, it was better than having him jam a garden hose up my backside and turn on the water, which is something else he enjoyed doing.

And he was still sending me into stores to ask the salesmen if they wanted a little action. Most of the time I could talk myself out of that situation, but not always. Once in North Miami, Chuck traded my services for a pair of high-powered binoculars. Another day, finding himself short of cash, Chuck negotiated a deal with an elderly florist. The old man was half undressed when his wife knocked on the door; she had been walking by and wanted to know why he was closing up shop in the middle of the day. Whenever something like that happened, I would feel that God had not forgotten me completely.

Everything Chuck thought of was designed to degrade me. And he always succeeded. I had come to think of myself as garbage. Whenever I found anything that was important to me, he simply destroyed it. It might be a simple thing, a suede belt with long fringes. I can still see him sitting there with a pair of scissors, calmly snipping sections off the belt. And just as he destroyed the belt, he sought to destroy any ties with other people.

Late one afternoon I was watching television and Chuck was lying on the bed cleaning his gun. There was a knock at the front door and he went to the window and looked out. My parents had shown up unexpectedly.

"Don't let them in yet," Chuck said. "Before you open the door, take off your robe."

"Chuck, those are my parents out there."

"Take off the robe."

"Chuck, don't do this to me."

"Take that robe off right now or I'll fucking rip it off you." He was pointing the gun at my head. "And now you open that fucking door. And if you let them know that this was my idea, I'm going to shoot you all. I mean that, Babe. All three of you will be fucking dead on the floor."

Naked, I walked to the door and opened it. I tried to stand out of the line of sight until my parents were in the room. My father turned a deep red and looked away, and my mother's mouth started to quiver. My parents had not seen me naked since I was a baby; it was terrible standing in front of them that way. No one said a word until Chuck decided to end the misery. He threw my robe to me.

"Put on something decent," he said. "How could you answer a door like that? You should have something on in front of your father."

It took my parents a few minutes to recover from this. Then, as it turned out, they had something on their minds.

"What did you want?" my mother asked.

"What do you mean?" I said.

"Well, you called us," she said. "What did you want?"

"What're you talking about? I didn't call you."

Chuck was glaring at me. But then he gave the matter some thought and he realized I couldn't have called. I hadn't been out of his sight the entire day; in fact, I hadn't had a chance to use a telephone in quite a few days.

"Your father told me that you'd called and you needed help."

"I didn't call."

"You called me," my father said. "You were crying and very disturbed and you told me to come over here right away because you needed my help."

"I don't know what you're talking about."

"Well, I got the phone call," he said. "And you were crying something awful. I got your mother at work and we both came right over here."

"It must have been a prank," Chuck said. "As you can see, there's nothing wrong here."

When my parents left that day, they left me with a riddle I've never been able to solve. There's only one person I know who sounds like me on the phone and that's my mother. I wonder whether she had sudden misgivings and, in hysterics, called my father. Or was it one of the other working girls, trying to do me a favor? I guess I'll never know.

I still hadn't been punished sufficiently for my escape to Betsy's house. When the punishment finally came, I didn't realize what was happening. I should have been suspicious when Chuck started fixing me up with a handsome, nine-teen-year-old garage mechanic named Tom. At first Chuck wouldn't let Tom near me; then, all of a sudden, I was told to be "extra nice" to Tom. I should have been on my guard when Chuck said that he wanted us to get together with Tom and his old lady, a hooker named Michelle.

Chuck was too interested in this Michelle. Whenever we went out for gas now, we stopped at the Hess service station where Tom worked and Chuck would always make con-versation with him. "How's Michelle?" he'd say. Or, "What's Michelle up to these days?"

This all seemed slightly peculiar to me. But then, there was little in my life that was *not* peculiar. So I didn't bother to try and figure it out. All I knew about Michelle was that she was a hooker, so I assumed Chuck was just doing some recruiting.

And Tom, I couldn't figure Tom at all. He was a good-looking boy—tall, blond, muscular—who could have gone out with nice girls and not paid a dime. Here he was, in his prime, living with one hooker and paying other hookers for their services.

And then, as Chuck began telling little stories about Michelle, I began to comprehend his fascination with her.

"You should do the kind of thing that Michelle does," he told me. "She's got this thing she does with shoes. She takes the trick's shoe and then she used the laces to tie the shoe around his balls. Then she plays 'Simon Says.' Every time he forgets to say, 'May I?', he has to jump up in the air with the shoe hanging from his balls. Tom told me about that one."

Tom and Chuck seemed to become closer friends, and

one day Chuck said that we were going to meet the famous Michelle. There was going to be a party at Michelle's house that night. I know that "party" usually means a place where people go to have fun. However, in those days it meant something else: it meant we'd be going somewhere to watch strange people do strange things to each other. I hadn't yet guessed that this was going to be my punishment for having tried to run away.

Michelle and Tom lived in the same neighborhood, about six blocks from Chuck's house. We parked our car outside a small house not much different from our own. As we approached the front door, Chuck stepped to one side and pushed me in front of him.

"You stand at the door," he said to me.

"Why do I have to stand at the door?"

"Michelle wants it that way."

At that, I started to back away but Chuck held me there. The door opened. A woman standing in the doorway reached out and took my hand.

"Here she is," Chuck said.

The woman looked angrily at Chuck, as though he had just spoken out of turn. However, by the time she looked back at me, all anger seemed gone from her eyes. She was still holding my hand in her own.

"And this must be Linda." A gentle voice. "Of course this is Linda. Linda, it's so good to see you."

Michelle was dressed entirely in black from her shoes to her throat. Her white skin seemed paler still against the blackness of her dress and her hair. When I looked at her, I thought of witches. She was thin and tall and at least ten years older than her Tom.

"Linda is here," she said to the others waiting in the living room. Tom was there, quiet, sitting in an easy chair. There was a young couple seated on the couch. He looked like a typical Joe College. They were to say very little all evening; they just sat quietly on the couch, looking so proper I wondered what they were doing at this "party."

I couldn't figure Chuck's role in all this. The setup seemed all wrong for him. The two other males in the room were young and virile. Also, he was taking a back seat while Michelle ran the whole show. This wasn't like Chuck.

"We don't want to punish you," Michelle was saying. "But whatever we do, it's for your own good. We *do* love you, Linda, and we're very happy that you've come back to us . . ."

I was only half-listening to Michelle as she slowly but surely got to the point. So it was going to be another of those nights. You might've thought that just once Chuck would take me someplace where there were normal people doing normal things, but that never happened.

"You were so cruel, Linda," Michelle was saying. "To have forsaken those who love you. Oh, the errors in judgment that young people make."

Why all this? Why the big production number? Was it all for my benefit, all to get me in the proper mood? Or was it for the benefit of the audience sitting quietly in the small living room waiting for the drama to unfold? Or was it—and this was the thought that bothered me the most—was it for her own benefit entirely? Was Michelle just turning herself on?

"Pardon me, Michelle," I said, "I don't mean to interrupt you, but I'm terribly thirsty."

"Thirsty? Oh, of course. You've had such a long journey that you must be terribly thirsty. Come into the kitchen and let me get you a soda."

She produced a can of soda from the refrigerator and I took a long cold drink.

"Linda, in a moment I'm going to ask you to remove your clothing," she said. "Would you prefer doing that here in the kitchen or out in the living room?"

"I'd prefer doing that nowhere."

"Oh, Linda, you're not being rude are you?" Even when we were alone, she went on with the act. That scared me. "Please don't disappoint me again. Please don't force me into making the punishment any more severe than it has to be."

"Michelle, I don't even know who you are."

*"Linda!"*

"I don't know you, and I never knew you," I said. "All I really know about you is that you're crazy. Do you know that? You're crazy and so's everyone else out there."

"Enough!" she said. "You're being very naughty now, Linda."

When Michelle led me back into the living room, I was naked. That fact didn't bother me all that much. By this time, there was no need to be self-conscious about that kind of thing. What bothered me was the unknown, the things that hadn't happened to me before. And I had no idea what these people were going to do to me. My thinking was "Okay, Linda, you're going to be in for a couple of hours of nuttiness here, so turn yourself numb, put all switches in the off position."

The faces looked eerie in the candlelight, but I still wasn't overly frightened. So much had happened to me that I couldn't conceive of anything too different. The main difference was the situation: this was my first time with a *woman* who was into S&M. But I'd been living with a man who seemed to know everything there was to know about sadism, and I couldn't see where this was going to be any worse. Okay, here comes the nuttiness; the nuttiness is about to start, and in an hour or two the nuttiness will all be over.

There was a small flash of fear. A hope that she was not way out there in Chuck's world. Michelle semed to sense my feeling.

"Don't be so frightened, my darling, Linda," she said. "This is going to hurt me more than it hurts you."

As she was talking to me and staring straight into my eyes, Michelle tied my hands together in front of me. Then she led me over to the couch, to a footrest in front of the couch. A miniature leather elephant. She bent me over the animal so that I was on my knees with my backside exposed to the rest of the room. Then I saw something in her hands. A whip, the kind of short stiff whip that jockeys use, a riding crop.

The setting reminded me, in a way, of church. A kind of flip-side church. The candles were flickering and the shadows on the wall were moving. It was like an altar set up in front of the parishioners. And me, I was the human sacrifice.

"Don't be alarmed." As Michelle spoke, she started tapping me gently here and there with the riding crop. "This is just the foreplay."

As Michelle went on tapping me, I began to relax. Some of my S&M tricks had been like that. They would pretend-hit you without ever inflicting real pain. Just love taps. At long as you pretended they were hurting you, as long as you cried out in make-believe pain, they would be satisfied. But I didn't like the word "foreplay." That might mean something else would be coming down later.

What came down almost immediately was a hair dryer, one of those hair dryers with a long snout. I've never even heard of this perversion before, and I'm sure Chuck's eyes were open wide. She began with the setting on warm, and she played the machine over my body. Everywhere. But still, there was no pain to speak of, not yet.

Michelle then switched the control up to hot, very hot, and, at the same time, she moved it across my body more and more slowly. And then she prodded me with it here and there, just letting it touch my skin before she pulled it away. The pain was real now but not unbearable. Michelle seemed to know just when to withdraw it, just when to pull it away and move it to another spot.

None of the others seemed to be participating in Michelle's ceremony of pain. I was bent into a position where I couldn't see them, but they weren't making a sound. The only way I knew they were still there was that Michelle would refer to them every now and then; she said they were there to bear witness to the punishment, to give testimony that justice was being done.

"And now, my dear Linda," Michelle said, "the foreplay is coming to an end. You must prepare yourself now for the . . . ah . . . true punishment. Before we begin, you must know that this is not personal, that we all love you very much and we're all happy to have you back among us again."

At this point, Michelle led me into a second room, a den. There was only one candle in this room. As the others found seats, I was bent over again, this time over the arm of a chair. The whip and the hair dryer had been left in the other room; this time her tool was to be a dildo.

"I only wish you were a man, not a girl," Michelle was saying. "I wouldn't do this to a girl unless she had been very naughty."

Then she began with the dildo. She prodded me with it gently at first and then she worked it into my rectum. This was not exactly a new experience; naturally, Chuck had done this many times in the past. Of all the things he made me do, this was one of the worst. I've always despised the insertion of any strange matter into my body. It had happened often enough so that I had devised a strategy for dealing with it. By this time I was familiar with my own pain threshold and I would begin shrieking before it hurt me seriously, before the real pain became too intense. My shrieks would cause Chuck to climax and leave me alone.

I had always been able to fool Chuck that way but Michelle was a different case. When I began screaming, she did not slow down. There was no way to fool her, and I was left with my last line of defense. I tried to adjust my body, to cut down on the pain through muscular control. Whenever she pushed into me, I'd move ever so slightly with the force. Even that didn't work. She compensated by pushing still harder.

Now I was screaming for real. Every now and then I caught a glimpse of Chuck. The candlelight glistened off the perspiration on his face. He was in a state of extreme excitement, so much so that it made me feel sick to my stomach. I had never seen that expression on his face; his face was *alive* with pleasure. You know, when you're making love to someone and you're in love with someone, the two of you will have very beautiful expressions on your face. He got that same expression on his face from watching that woman rip into me.

Occasionally, Chuck would look away from me and stare at Michelle. His expression changed to one of great admiration. He had finally met someone who knew more about administering pain than he did.

When I tried to squirm away from Michelle and her dildo, Chuck complained.

"She's trying to back off."

"You shut up!" She was a wildcat screeching at Chuck. "I'm taking care of her now and *you just fuck off!* This is my work, this is me."

As she screamed at Chuck, she was stabbing into me faster and faster, harder and harder. My numbness defense mechanism was no longer functioning. There was a short circuit in my *Off* switch and I panicked. Not just from the pain, although this was the most intense pain I'd known. But suddenly I had the feeling that Michelle had slipped over the edge of sanity and there would be no way of stopping her until I was lying there dead. I was sure she would stab at me and rip at me with that dildo until there was nothing left of me.

"Oh, God!" I called out. "Stop her! Make her stop! She's killing me!"

Michelle was clearly in a high state of excitement herself, sobbing out her breaths. But it got worse and worse, always worse. She had both hands on the dildo now and she was stabbing it into me. Then I felt the warmth of blood gushing out my rectum. There was no way to stop the pain and there was no way to stop her.

Finally, someone did speak up. It was the other male in the room. Joe College. Until that moment he had not said a single word. And when he finally did say something, I was feeling faint from the loss of blood.

"Whoa! Whoa right there," he said. "What the hell are you doing to this chick?"

I was astonished. All the things I had been involved in—everything that had happened to me up to then—I had never heard anyone else stand up and say that it was wrong or crazy. When I realized that he was on his feet, my only fear was that he'd leave before stopping Michelle. But no, he walked over to the high priestess and grabbed her arm.

"That's all," he said. "We're ending this right now. You fucking people are crazy. We're going to get this girl to a hospital right now."

Michelle seemed to have some trouble hearing him. It was as if she was coming out of a heavy trance. She had been getting off on the blood.

"Yes," she said, finally. "I suppose that is enough punishment."

"I'm going to call the hospital," the young man said.

"No, I can handle this." Michelle seemed back in full control of herself. "I've got just the things to take care of this. Don't worry about it. It's nowhere near as serious as it appears."

"Yeah, don't get in an uproar," Chuck chimed in. "Linda loves this. She does this kind of thing all the time."

Michelle then produced a jar of some kind of ointment and she rubbed that into my wound. It seemed to stop the bleeding.

"Sometimes the punishment will hurt a little," Michelle cooed. "But it hurts me just as much. It's just that we must be sure that you don't run away again. We wouldn't want to hear of you doing anything naughty again."

I was so grateful that the pain was coming to an end. It was the worst pain ever. I would have much rather been punched and kicked by Chuck than have had Michelle sticking that thing into me.

"If this gives you any more trouble," Michelle was saying,

"you should check into a hospital for a day or two. But it won't. It'll clear up, and you'll be as good as new."

As we drove home that night, Chuck seemed angry with me.

"You had to go bleed and ruin everything," he said.

"What?"

"Your fucking bleeding," he said. "That Michelle was just getting into it when you started bleeding all over the place."

"You're blaming me for *bleeding?*"

"It's the way you were fucking doing it," he said. "Your whole fucking attitude. You couldn't look like you were enjoying it a little? You couldn't beg for more? On, no. Not you. And that other guy, that fag, he has to go and open his mouth. Take you to the *hospital*—where's that guy been all his life?"

The evening may not have gone perfectly for Chuck but remembering it later on brought him no end of pleasure. The mere act of remembering was enough to set Chuck off again.

"I wonder what Michelle is doing tonight," he'd say. "She was really some piece of work, that Michelle. Remember that night we were over at her house and she tied you up— remember that?—and she was coming at you with that fucking dildo? God, that was some night."

# *fourteen*

Chuck put me through so many degrading scenes, so many Michelles, that I'm sure people wonder why I didn't find a way to murder him. Well, the thought *did* cross my mind. But whenever I was filled with the resolve to kill him, there was no way to do it. And when there was a way, there was no will.

Once one of my tricks gave me some poison pills; he said that two of the pills in a glass of water would kill a person in just a few minutes. I kept those pills for days while I thought about it. That was one inner battle I almost lost. But finally I flushed the pills away. There were other times when Chuck would have a diabetic seizure; I could've just left him on the floor, just walked away, but something stopped me.

No matter how evil a person is, I couldn't just walk away and let him die. I could never be the cause of someone else's being killed. I have always believed in God and I knew that God would get me out of my troubles. I know today that God will take care of Chuck without any help from me or anyone else. If people do bad all the time, they're going to suffer.

However, back then it seemed as if God was looking the other way. Chuck and Michelle had been evil; yet, I was the one who suffered. And the suffering was getting worse. Several days after the "party," an infection set in and began hurting. When the hurting became unbearable, Chuck finally came up with a doctor for me, a proctologist I'll call Dr. James.

Dr. James was short, about fifty years old and he wore heavy horn rimmed glasses. He completed his examination quickly.

"You have an infection," he said. "Nothing we can't take care of. But let me tell you something, you shouldn't fool around like that any more. I must be blunt—you should have no more anal sex."

I couldn't have agreed more heartily. I wanted to tell him that this wasn't my idea in the first place. But, as usual, I said nothing. What would he have thought? What would he have said if he knew the infection had come from some maniacal woman stabbing me with a dildo?

"If you don't stop the practice of anal sex," he said, taking on an almost fatherly tone, "this will cause you a great deal of pain. And that's not the worst of it. There will come a time some day when you will lose control of your muscles there, the sphincter muscles, and you won't be able to regulate your bowel movements. Believe me, I've seen it happen. This is a not uncommon phenomenon among older members of the homosexual community. But what is bothering you now is the pain; I think you should look on the pain as a warning."

"Doctor, do me one favor. Don't tell my husband about the pain, about the anal sex causing me pain."

"But surely he's just the one I *should* tell."

"No, really, Doc," I said. "Just don't tell my husband. If he knows it hurts me, he'll just go on doing it. I've got to tell you, he's a little weird that way."

The doctor guided me back out to the waiting room, and Chuck whispered to me.

"Did you work out a deal?"

"What?"

"A deal—what kind of a deal did you work out for the bill?"

"Chuck, he's a *doctor!*"

"Oh, Doc!" Chuck raised his voice. "My old lady tells me she didn't work out a deal for the bill yet."

"No, we haven't discussed payment," the doctor said.

Chuck took the doctor to one side and their whispered discussion lasted no more than a minute or two. As Chuck came over to me, he gave me a wink and a smile. The meaning was clear. Chuck was not going to have to pay for the bill; I was. Not in cash but in services. It was to be a professional service for a professional service.

"Your appointment will be one week from today." The doctor's attitude was very matter-of-fact. "I'll see you at the end of the working day. Just after my nurse leaves. Let's see now, you'll be the last appointment of the day. There'll be no one else here. No, no, I'll tell you what. Before coming, call me first at this number—that way you can be sure everyone has gone. That should do it for now. It was nice meeting you, Mr. and Mrs. Traynor."

"Yeah, so long, Doc," Chuck said. "See you Thursday."

"Oh, there's one more thing," the doctor said. "Mr. Traynor, I've already told your wife this: No more anal sex. Any more anal sex will cause her a great deal of pain."

"Right," Chuck said, smiling.

What kind of world do we live in? Would you believe that a doctor, a professional man, would accept sexual favors as payment for a bill? I would assume that a doctor would ask you whether you had Blue Cross or Blue Shield or medical insurance, but I never heard that kind of question from a doctor. No, they listened to Chuck for just a minute and the only question they would ask me was whether I could see them after regular office hours. I guess this shouldn't have surprised me; it happened often enough.

The only good thing to come out of my meeting with Dr.

James was a prescription for *Percodan*. When Chuck asked me what the pills were for, I didn't bother mentioning their pain-killing properties. I told Chuck they were supposed to reduce the infection. As you might imagine, Chuck had only negative feelings about pain killers. And I sensed that *Percodan* could make life a good deal easier for me. I managed to hide most of the pills from Chuck and use them as necessary. If I got a vial of several dozen *Percodan* pills, I'd empty out most of them and let Chuck see only a half dozen of them.

Every Thursday afternoon, Dr. James went through an examination that seemed quicker than the week before. And then he'd give me some *Percodan* pills out of his drawer with a hand that trembled slightly.

"Everything looks fine," he'd say. "Just fine. Let's go inside."

After leading me into a second office, he locked the door, sat down, unzippered himself, and waited for me. The tricks always found a way to let me know just what they wanted. If they undressed themselves, they wanted intercourse. The ones who just unzippered themselves wanted oral sex. Dr. James was nervous throughout the process, constantly glancing toward the locked door of his inner office, anxious to dismiss me as soon as he had finished.

"See you next week," he'd say.

At this time, Dr. James was one of four professional men I was servicing in a single office complex in downtown Miami. In addition to the proctologist, I was visiting a dermatologist on a regular basis. And, when Chuck developed eye trouble, he added an optometrist to our list. And, finally, there was a former lawyer of Chuck's. I found it absolutely amazing that so many professionals would be so willing to trade services. And I also found myself praying that Chuck and I stayed in good health.

The dermatologist—his real name is Dr. Gross—supplied Chuck with pill prescriptions, either ups or downs, in exchange for me. Chuck always liked to have plenty of pills around to give as favors to the girls who worked for him.

Dr. Gross, a young man still in his thirties, always seemed to be in a good mood. One reason for his high spirits might have been the nurses who worked for him: he seemed to have surrounded himself with nurses who had unusually large and perky breasts. When Chuck commented on this one day, he learned that Dr. Gross had given his nurses silicone injections. Chuck decided that would be just the thing for me. But first he asked one of the nurses what the breasts were like.

"Do they feel natural, or do they get hard?"

"Why don't you feel for yourself?"

Naturally, Chuck needed no further encouragement. I had to wonder at that. Was the nurse such a tramp? Or was it possible that her breasts had lost their sensitivity? Something else bothered me about the whole thing. I learned that it was illegal to have silicone injected into your breasts. It seems to me when something is illegal, there's usually a danger connected with it.

Dr. Gross pointed out one of the drawbacks himself. He said that if I used silicone, I'd never be able to breastfeed a baby. I would never agree to something that would interfere with that. Even then I clung to the belief that someday I was going to have a normal life. I was going to marry and have children and those children were going to feed from me in a natural way.

I think every woman dreams about having beautiful, large, well-shaped breasts, but the notion of silicone terrified me. It was connected somehow to my feeling about dildoes. Because I can't stand the thought of any unnatural object being placed into my body, I certainly didn't want them injecting any chemical—or whatever it was—inside of my breasts.

However, the decision was not mine to make. Chuck decided that I would be better off with bigger breasts. And if that meant I could never nurse a baby—well, so what? What would that ever mean to him?

Dr. Gross informed Chuck that this was too big an operation to do in exchange for services; he would require cash. Chuck agreed and, needless to say, the cash was raised through my professional services.

This, then, was one of the few times I visited a doctor during his office hours. That first day I was scared to death. I was lying on a table and he began with injections of pain killer. Then he produced a huge needle, a tube filled with a gel substance. It looked like something from a cartoon, something you might use for knocking out a horse or decorating a cake.

The gigantic needles were shoved into all four sides of each breast; that awful stuff was pumped right into me. Despite the early pain-killing injections, the insertion of the silicone was extremely painful.

At first, while I was still lying flat on my back, I didn't notice any difference. But when I got to my feet, I could see the change. That quickly I went from a size 34-B to a size 36-C. Although my breasts did appear much fuller, I had the feeling they no longer belonged to me.

Chuck kept looking at the new me in disbelief. And I must admit, my new breasts gave me a temporary break from Chuck's abuse. His favorite descriptive phrase for me had always been "flat-chested." Now he was at a loss for words. He would find other failings in time, but at least for a few days there was a breather.

Chuck was able to accept the new breasts more easily than I could. In the years to come, as I heard more and more about the dangers of silicone, I began to realize that Dr. Gross had put time bombs into my breasts. And, in fact, the time bombs went off a few years ago. What happened was that the silicone did not stay together. It separated, slipping here and there, and my breasts became lumpy and painful. A doctor in California decided that my breasts had to be removed at once. He said that later it might be possible to do reconstructive surgery, putting in implants and building them up all over again.

I waited a week and went to another doctor. He said that what was happening was that my milk glands were starting to swell up and that I was going to have a baby. Fortunately, that doctor was correct. I did have my baby. And there was a second pleasant surprise—I was able to nurse him.

Since then, I've seen other doctors. I've been warned that the disintegrating silicone could form a clot that could kill me. I've also been told the breasts should still come off. But I don't have much faith in doctors anymore.

# *fifteen*

---

The beginnings of fame. A few customers said they had seen me in a movie up in New York. And occasionally a trick would ask me to "deep-throat" him. Then, one day in late summer of 1972, we got a telephone call from Lou Perry. He said that he would pay all travel expenses if we would come up to New York and be interviewed.

However, before we took that trip, Chuck decided to buy a little present for me. A dog.

On a terribly hot day toward the end of summer, Chuck took me to the Humane Society so I could help him pick out a proper pet. He asked me to select one that I liked. I chose a cute little female Cocker Spaniel, but this was not what Chuck had in mind. Not at all. What Chuck had in mind was Rufus, a two-year-old mix of Bloodhound and Great Dane, an oversized, sad-faced mutt.

Chuck, of course, was into perversions, not pets. While he kept Rufus chained out in the backyard, he spent a great deal of time telling me exactly why he had gotten me a dog like Rufus. It was, as you've guessed, to expand my sexual horizons in what was, to me, the most painful possible way.

"Now take off your clothes while I get the dog," he said. "It's important that you two get to know each other."

I was scared to death. But I was resolved that this encounter with a dog would not turn out like the last one. And this time I had some help, some expert advice. A hooker who had specialized in making love to dogs told me just what to do to make it work—and, at the same time, just what *not* to do.

"The whole thing is this," she had told me, "you've got to wait for the animal to come to you. Stay in just one spot and let him take all the time in the world. If you move at all, he may get scared off. A dog doesn't like it when you back away or make any moves toward it."

"Really?" I had said.

"Oh, yeah, never do that. And whatever else you do, don't touch it directly. You'll scare the dog to death."

Clearly, all I had to do was reverse her instructions. I imagine both Rufus and Chuck were befuddled when I came on like gangbusters. Rufus was interested, but only to a point. The minute I made a move toward him, he backed off.

Chuck watched all this unbelievingly. He couldn't complain about my performance—there I was, aggressive to a fault, looking like I wanted nothing else on earth but to make love to this dog. And Rufus looked like an out-and-out quitter.

"There must be something really wrong with you," Chuck decided. "You are so fucking ugly that even a fucking animal won't fuck you."

Another small victory. Anyway, as we left for New York and the first round of interviews, I was in an up mood. Neither Chuck nor I could imagine why any newspaper would want to interview someone who had been in a hard core porno movie. But neither of us knew that *Deep Throat* was being treated as something more than a routine dirty movie. We had no idea that *Screw*, the sex newspaper, had called it "the very best porno ever made". And we didn't know that customers were lining up around the World Theatre on Manhattan's West 49th Street to see the most talked-about film of the year.

Chuck had a prediction: We would be interviewed by a

couple of the sex papers and then, in a week or so, it would all blow away.

"I don't want to use the name 'Traynor' in any interviews," he said. "We don't want the whole fucking family down on our asses. From now on you use the name from the movie, Lovelace. You are Linda Lovelace. And I am J.R., your husband and manager."

"J.R.?"

"Right, you got it. I am not Traynor and I am not Chuck. From now on, it is J.R."

On the flight to New York, Chuck made up complete new identities for us. I was twenty-one years old, not twenty-three. He was a New York City photographer, and he discovered me in my home town of Bryan, Texas. He chose Bryan, Texas, because he had once worked there and he knew how many stores there were, and where the nearest movie theater was. He said it was a flat little town; you could stand in the center of town and see everything there was to see by just turning slowly around.

"If they ask you what your parents think about what you're doing, you say that doesn't matter—you're doing this because you want to do it. That's the key thing: You *want* to do it; you *like* doing it. Get this straight, Linda. These people think you're the turn-on Queen of all time. Just this once, start acting it. Anyone asks you why you suck cock, you love it. That's what turns you on."

Chuck went over every question I might be asked and then he told me the answers I was supposed to give. If someone asked me a question we hadn't gone over, I was supposed to wait until Chuck chimed in with the right answer.

Sample question: *Does it bother you to suck cock in front of so many people?*

Sample answer: *Oh, no, I love it. I guess I'm what you might call an exhibitionist.*

Sample question: *Do you think you could take twelve inches?*

Sample answer: *Oh, sure, no problem.*

Sample question: *Which is better, sex with men or sex with women?*

Sample answer: *Sex with both—I can never get enough of either one.*

I wasn't at all surprised to learn that the one who really enjoyed the interviews was Chuck. He loved stepping in and answering all the questions. He finally had a chance to tell the world everything he felt about life. He could talk about Nixon politics (bad) and prudes (bad) and far-out sex (good). He even gave me a whole speech to memorize about censorship (very bad). And now I became his puppet, mouthing everything he wanted the world to hear.

"People should be free to do whatever they want to do," I said at least a million times. "They should be free, unrestricted, uninhibited, and open-minded."

The only thing that upset Chuck was when I was asked a question that didn't focus in on my sexual talent or, worse, a question totally unrelated to sex. Then I was supposed to turn the question around: "Do you always ask such boring questions?" or "Can't you think of something more exciting to ask?"

"Any newspaper guy hints at anything," Chuck said, "or if he asks you to do anything, you just do it, and right away."

That was Chuck's complete thinking on the subject of public relations. An effective publicity program, like everything else in life, was built around sexual activity.

"But why do they want to talk with me?" I asked Chuck.

"Search me," he said.

The producers knew why. But then the producers had the weekly box office receipts. They knew that in just the World Theater the picture would gross nearly a million-and-a-half dollars before being closed down by the authorities. They also had the accumulating interview requests, not just from sleaze-sheets like *Screw* but from newspapers like the *New York Daily News*. They knew of the magazines that were doing articles and the fact that *Playboy* was anxious for a photo spread.

I began to sense what was happening the first time we saw producer Lou Perry. Suddenly it was, "You're looking well, Linda" and "How's life been treating you, Linda?" It was hard to believe that this was the same man who wanted me fired off the set because I was "ruining" his movie.

Our first official interview was with *Screw* and we had been told that since that publication was largely responsible for *Deep Throat*'s success, we were to be very cooperative. Whatever *Screw* wanted, *Screw* was to get. And the two men responsible for *Screw*, editor Al Goldstein and publisher Jim Buckley, were both going to be there for the interview.

When I put on my regular clothes, blue jeans and a blouse, Chuck decided that wasn't good enough for the editors of *Screw*. Chuck had recently purchased three or four transparent blouses, and I wore one of them whenever he wanted to demonstrate the wonders of silicone. And so for *Screw* it was a transparent blouse, no bra.

I was immediately struck by the contrast between the two men. You could tell that Goldstein was a cheap guy—loud, crude, rude, infantile, obnoxious, and dirty. His partner Buckley seemed a contrast: neat and clean, sensitive, and quiet. Buckley observed me closely. Just from the way he looked at me, I got the feeling that he knew what was happening.

The interview itself was filthy and silly:

> *"What's the largest cock you've ever sucked?"* I was asked. *"Is it the guy in the film, or has there been somebody so large that you couldn't get it all in?"*
>
> "No," I said. *"That's never happened. Nobody has ever been too large or too wide or anything."*
>
> *"Once your throat opens, your esophagus gets quite large, like a sword-swallower's."* Chuck was right there to offer the full scientific explanation. *"You've seen some sword-swallowers putting three-foot swords down. It's the same thing."*

"*Do you breathe through your nose?*" I was asked.

"*You have to breathe through your mouth,*" I said, "*so whoever's going in my throat has to work in and out. As they come out I take a breath.*"

"*Do you come even though your clit isn't being worked on?*"

"*Yeah, I do,*" I said. "*I have an orgasm every time I get screwed in the throat.*"

I could tell by Chuck's smile that I was doing all right. I was amazed that they would be asking me the same kind of questions that Chuck had rehearsed with me. The same questions would be asked by reporters from many sleazy publications, and my answers never varied at all.

"*Do you enjoy the taste of sperm?*" Goldstein asked me.

"*Oh, yeah, I do. I love it. It's caviar to me. I can't understand why other chicks get so totally turned off by it. I never spit it out.*"

"*How would you describe the taste?*"

"*I really couldn't describe the taste . . . you'd have to taste it. Try it.*"

Goldstein was asking more and more questions about the act itself—how did it taste and how did it feel and how did I think it made a man feel and so on. Since I wasn't taking the hint, Chuck did.

"Well, why don't you find out for yourself?" Chuck said. "You want a free sample, help yourself."

The editor of Screw almost tripped over his own feet racing over to the bed. As I did it to Goldstein, I could hear Chuck ask Buckley whether he'd like a sample, too.

"No, thanks," Buckley said.

Although Goldstein was a pig, I could numb myself to that experience. But it was harder to numb myself to the new phenomenon of being interviewed. At first I thought it wouldn't matter what I said. So what if I spouted Chuck's words and thoughts? Who would believe that stuff anyway? And those words weren't mine. They were words being delivered by the Linda Lovelace doll. That was the first I'd thought of myself as the Linda Lovelace doll and it might have been the result of a joke I had just heard ("Did you hear about the Linda Lovelace doll? Wind it up and it swallows the key").

During the next few days, Chuck wound up the Linda Lovelace doll and she gave interviews. Although there was one more scene like the scene with Goldstein, most interviewers were decent people and would not respond to Chuck's hints or invitations. I realized that interviews didn't all have to be bad. As long as I was answering questions, I didn't have to be a hooker. And as long as I was being interviewed, I was able to eat in restaurants that Chuck would never have otherwise entered. The *New York Daily News* interview the next day was in a fancy Manhattan restaurant where the food was so tasty, I couldn't keep my mind on the questions.

Nothing else really changed that much, not at first anyway. Chuck explained that Lou Perry was negotiating for another movie, a sequel, and that I should be taking care of the producer as long as we were in New York. So I did. It was no longer a curt, "Lock the door." Now it was, "Oh, Linda, would you mind locking the door behind you?" The general attitude toward me had changed but everything else was the same.

The movie was breaking records everywhere, so we spent a lot of time in Lou Perry's office talking about the next one, *Deep Throat, Part II*. One day while we were there, Lou's office phone rang. His secretary told him that the caller was Sammy Davis, Jr.

At first I thought it was a joke. What would a big star like Sammy Davis have to say to someone like Lou? But judging from Lou's side of the conversation, the two of them —the superstar and the producer of dirty movies—were old friends. Stranger still, Sammy Davis was talking to Lou about *Deep Throat*. Apparently he had enjoyed the movie so much that he wanted to borrow a print to show in his home.

"Sure, Sammy, we can take care of that," Lou said. There was a pause in Lou's side of the conversation and he swiveled around and looked at me. I gathered that my name had just entered the talk. "Yeah, sure, I know her. As a matter of fact, I know her very well. Hey, you want to know where she is right now? Two feet away. That's right. Listening to every word. Sammy, would I kid you?"

Lou listened for a few more minutes, then cupped his hand over the telephone mouthpiece and whispered over to me.

"Hey, would you fuck a nigger?"

I shook my head no but even as I was doing that, Chuck overruled me.

"Sure she would," he said.

"Sure, Sammy, she'd *love* to meet you. Hey, she's looking forward to it. Right, we'll have her over there tonight. Why not?"

That night as Lou's bodyguard, Vinnie, drove us over to the Waldorf Astoria, I started to worry about my clothes. What would a big star like Sammy Davis think when he saw the way I was dressed? Jeans and an army jacket. Chuck, too, seemed a little tense. But Sammy Davis Jr. was one of the biggest celebrities of them all.

"I want to see something happen tonight," Chuck told me. "If Sammy drops any kind of a hint, pick up on it right away. I don't want you waiting until I say something."

"Chuck, this is *Sammy Davis Junior!*"

"And you're Linda Lovelace. So what's that mean? Listen, he's got to be some kind of a freak. He wouldn't have gone fucking ape for *Deep Throat* if he wasn't into that shit. I want to see you coming on with him. Any suggestion he makes, any kind of scene he's got in mind, I want you to hop right into it."

As excited as I was about meeting the star, I was also a

little scared. What if Chuck was right? I had been flattered by the thought that he wanted to meet me and now that same thought troubled me. *Why* did he want to meet me so much? The only thing he really knew about me was that I was the main freak in a freak show called *Deep Throat*. And why was someone like Sammy Davis watching that piece of trash in the first place?

Chuck could not have been more wrong. When we arrived at Sammy's hotel suite, he was in the company of his wife, Altovise, who was doing needlepoint work. The whole time we were there, she did her needlepoint and Sammy did the talking.

All that first night, Sammy talked movies with us. He had a cassette player with him and he entertained us by putting on a tape of *West Side Story*.

"Do you remember that great dance sequence in the first part of *West Side Story*?" he asked, turning on the machine. "You've got to see this. It was done in one take and it's really going to knock your eyes out."

Chuck yawned, fidgeted, cracked his knuckles, did everything he could to show that the evening was not following the design he had in mind. Nothing happened. Nothing. We sat there for two hours and Sammy didn't mention a single sexy subject. He talked about two things—old movies and the television show he was doing the next day, the Highway Safety Telethon. Chuck was about as fascinated with the Highway Safety Telethon as he was in Altovise's needlepoint. But I found it interesting.

"You know, I could be on that telethon," I said at one point. "I was in an automobile accident a couple of years ago and it came close to killing me. I could tell people they should always remember their seat belts."

"That'd be a gas," Sammy said. "Hey, you know what, I *like* it! Linda Lovelace on the telethon. And all you'd have to do is describe what happened to you and how people should be like more careful."

"I don't know if this is such a cool idea," Chuck said. "Then everyone'll know that you've got scars all over your body."

"Well, it's up to you," Sammy said.

"I'd really like to do it," I said.

"Then it's settled."

Maybe a Highway Safety Telethon doesn't sound all that exciting. Perhaps you'll have trouble understanding why I was so anxious to do it. Because it was decent. Because it was respectable. Because I wouldn't have to take off my clothes. I can't tell you how pleased I was that night. Who would have guessed that a great entertainer like Sammy Davis Jr. would treat me with such respect?

Not until the next night did that first taste of fame go sour. It was then that I learned it's one thing to be a famous actress, say, a Jane Fonda, and it's quite another thing to be a Linda Lovelace.

I dressed with care for my television debut. Normal clothes —a black skirt and a blue blouse. And I kept going over in my mind what I was going to say. I was going to describe my own accident—not all the gory details, but enough so that people would know how serious it was. Then I would point out that things might have gone better for me if only I had remembered to fasten my seat belt.

Sammy's wife, Altovise, was waiting for us at the entrance to the theater. Although she was extremely sweet with me, all the sweetness in the world couldn't soften the blow.

"Come along," she said. "I'll show you the way to the dressing room. Sammy will be along in a minute or two. He wants to tell you himself how disappointed he is that you won't be able to do the television show."

"Oh, I can do it. I'm all ready."

"I can see that," Altovise said. "But the women who own the theater—they're just letting us use it for the telethon— they say you can't go on stage. They tell us that if we use you, then we can forget about using the theater."

"But I'll—"

"I'm sorry, Linda," she said. "Sammy doesn't want any hassles."

I was shattered. The women were upset by someone who really wasn't me, but I was the one who would do the suffering. Not that other person. Not that Linda Lovelace doll. What would she care about a Highway Safety Telethon? On top of the rejection, there was a feeling of helplessness— there was no way to tell those people that Linda Lovelace and I were two different people. I pretended that it didn't matter to me, and that was the only acting I was to do that night.

Sammy was all apologies and he insisted that we join him for dinner. It was then that I began to see what it means to be a celebrity. A Sammy Davis Jr. doesn't just walk into a restaurant and eat dinner. No, for him there's a special room upstairs, a private dining room, a long table by a window, service and food that regular patrons will never see.

A Sammy Davis Jr. doesn't just sit down and order a quiet dinner for two. As he sits down, the chairs around him fill with people, his people. The bodyguard. Two secretaries. The hangers-on. All told, seven or eight people to protect him, to love him, to laugh along with him, to tell him how good he is, to eat his food. And we were just like the rest, one of Sammy's coterie, enjoying the first tastes of fame and first tastes of food I didn't know existed.

Sammy arranged the seating, placing me in the spot of honor right next to him. Putting Altovise beside Chuck Traynor. Sammy and me. Chuck and Altovise. It would become more in time, more than just a seating arrangement.

# *sixteen*

---

Suddenly there was money and the prospect of more money to come. *Deep Throat, Part II* would bring Chuck a huge chunk of money. I forget the exact amount because it wasn't important to me; I'd never see any of it anyway. And then *Playboy* was paying for me to fly to California and pose for a picture spread. Again, I'm not sure about the money part. But it was enough so that Chuck's attitude toward me began to change.

Chuck couldn't get over the fact that a big celebrity like Sammy Davis Jr. wanted to know me. He again seemed surprised that a big magazine like *Playboy* would pay good money for pictures of me. Chuck realized he had a hot property on his hands though he didn't yet know how much that property would be worth.

No longer did Chuck make me go into stores and proposition salesmen. He stopped making me strip in cars and flash at diners. And he even stopped yelling at me so much. He seemed as though he were a little dazed by it all, like a kid being taken to Disneyland for the first time.

I noticed this especially during our first trip to California to make the *Playboy* layout. We were driven everywhere in a limousine with a chauffeur. Our first stop was a huge estate with rolling lawns and imposing gates. The limo came to a halt beside a booth with security guards.

I heard the words, "We have Miss Linda Lovelace," and—open sesame!—the gates swung open and we were on a driveway that seemed as long as a country road. At the end of the driveway, atop a hill, sat Playboy Mansion West. It looked like an English castle, or at least the way I thought an English castle should look. A huge stone mansion with a slate roof and ivy crawling up the sides and trees pressing in against it. At that time, of course, it was just a place to me, a place to work. I had no idea that in time the mansion would become my second home.

The prospect of the work itself didn't bother me at all. I'd seen several copies of *Playboy* and I knew I'd be wearing few, if any, clothes. The silicone in my breasts had not yet started to break down so I wasn't too self-conscious. And I knew that there'd be no whips or dildoes used as photographic props.

The photographer waiting for us at the mansion was courteous and gentlemanly. The contrast between him and the other photographers I'd worked with was remarkable. He had decided on a theme for his photographs; he was going to use lace—as in Love-*lace*—and he had gone to dozens of antique shops looking for beautiful old lace. Then he commented on my hair, saying that he loved the way the sunlight reflected off my hair. Just the way he talked to me made me feel relaxed and even a little beautiful.

The Playboy Mansion West was as impressive inside as it was outside. Huge floor-to-ceiling windows set in rock, gigantic fireplaces, leather couches, a beautiful library with backgammon tables and, everywhere, butlers running around carrying trays. The pool itself was a separate world. Have you ever seen a pool with its own waterfall? One could swim under the waterfall and come out in a cave-like room with a second pool, a huge Jacuzzi, piped-in music, and colored lights. In time I would get to know the full Playboy layout—

the greenhouse, the tennis courts, the bath house, the whole fantasy.

Everyone in the place treated me as though I was someone special. One of the photographer's assistants put body makeup all over me. And the photographer didn't just snap his pictures and move on; he worked hard for special dramatic effects. He made some pictures where the sun provided backlighting. He posed me beside a tree and in the company of a stone lion, usually with yards of lace draped over my body. True, he asked me to strike some absurd poses—licking my lips with my tongue, touching my breasts, sucking my finger—but these things weren't too upsetting, not really, not when I considered what other photographers had made me do.

It was a giant step up. The shooting went on most of the day and when it was over, I had a visitor, Joanie, the private secretary to Hugh Hefner, the publisher of *Playboy*.

"Miss Lovelace, Mr. Hefner would like you to come back to the mansion tonight," she said. "There's going to be a buffet and a movie."

Chuck answered the invitation.

"You can tell Mr. Hefner that we'd both be delighted to come," he said.

The secretary looked at her clipboard.

"I'm sorry," she said. "I've only got Miss Lovelace's name down here."

"Well, Linda does not go anywhere without me," Chuck said. "If I don't go, then she don't go."

"I'll have to check on that."

Which she did. The secretary returned almost immediately with the word that it would be fine if we both wanted to come that evening. Chuck could hardly wait. The rest of that day, as we were getting ready for the party, he kept telling me what a big deal *Playboy* was. To me, *Playboy* was just the magazine that my brother-in-law used to read in the bathroom, nothing more than that. To Chuck, it was a very

big deal. How big? 'This big: Chuck decided that my usual
army-surplus wardrobe was not going to be quite grand
enough for the people who would be at the mansion that
night. He took the unprecedented step of actually going out
and buying me a dress, a beautiful, gray, knitted dress that
buttoned down the front and clung to my body like an extra-
long sweater. And for once, he didn't try to negotiate a sexual
trade with the salesman. Nope, he walked right into a nice
store on Sunset Strip, picked out a nice dress, and paid almost
$100.00 in cash for it. This was big.

That was what I was wearing that night when the *Playboy*
limousine picked us up and drove us back to the mansion.
The huge living room had been converted into a small theater;
a movie screen came down over the front windows and a
projector was concealed in the walls between the living room
and the library. Fifty or sixty people were there to see the
movie that night.

I can no longer remember what the movie was, or who
starred in it, but whoever they were, they could not have
been more impressive than the stars who were there to watch
the movie. It was there, at the Playboy Mansion West, that
I first met Warren Beatty and Goldie Hawn and Elizabeth
Taylor and Connie Stevens and James Caan and Peter Law-
ford, and many more. And they, of course, met Linda Lovelace. But that's not entirely true. In many cases, I wouldn't
even speak to the people. Take someone like Elizabeth
Taylor, for example—when I saw someone like that, someone
so important to my own life, I was ashamed to even think
about meeting her. I knew what she would think of me. I
mean, how could she help it? And why on earth would someone like that even want to meet me?

Thinking back, I can't even remember what *kind* of movie
they showed that first night. One reason my memory might
be so bad is that I was thinking about the man who had
chosen the seat next to mine. Clint Eastwood. *Clint Eastwod!*
When he came into the room and took the seat right next
to my own, I thought I'd die. When I was growing up, I never

missed his television show, *Rawhide*. My bedroom wall was
decorated with many famous faces but my two favorites were
Elvis and Clint Eastwood. And here he was, in real life. He
didn't say a single word to me all evening. I give him credit
for that. In fact, it made me respect him even more.

At the end of the movie, when the living room lights came
on, we were again visited by Hugh Hefner's secretary, Joanie.

"If you've got a minute," she said, "Mr. Hefner would
like to meet you."

Then, as the celebrities and other guests headed for the
dessert or the swimming pool, Chuck and I went for our
first meeting with Hugh Hefner. I had no image of the magazine publisher at that time. All I knew about him was that
he was high on Chuck's list of all-time important people. And,
as we went to meet him, Chuck whispered last-minute instructions in my ear. This was to become the usual celebrity
briefing: If he wanted sexual favors of any kind, I was to
be quick in offering them.

Hefner greeted us politely. He seemed quiet but sure of
himself. In the weeks and months that followed, I would get
to know Hefner better, too much better, but my own first
impressions were positive ones. He complimented me, saying
that I was prettier in person than on a movie screen. Then
he said that he thought *Deep Throat* was an excellent movie,
one he had screeened several times at the mansion. The
reason he liked it, he said, was that it was not just straight
sex—he said that it had a story and a comic point of view.

Thereafter, the two men tended to keep me out of the
conversation. I know it must seem as though I don't have
much to say during many of these encounters. Well, that
happens to be the truth. I was the reason that Hefner and
Chuck got together, but I was not someone they talked to
or with. I was someone they talked about.

Then Hefner said that while he liked *Deep Throat*, he
was more interested by the movie I'd made with a dog.

"Oh, you saw that one?" Chuck said.

"Oh, that was terrific," Hefner said. "You know, we've

tried that several times, tried to get a girl and a dog together, but it has never worked out."

"Yeah, that can be very tricky," Chuck said. "The chick's got to know what she's doing."

"That's something I'd like to see," Hefner said. "I think I've seen every animal flick ever made but—"

"You'd like to see that?" Chuck said. "Hey, no sweat. That's no big deal for Linda."

Hefner was a collector of eight-millimeter movies. He supposedly has the second largest collection in the world, second only to someone in Singapore. His eight-millimeter movies go back to the first ones ever made, and they include some with actors and actresses who were to go on and become very famous. He seemed especially interested in his animal films; pigs, chickens, donkeys, horses—he had them all.

For the next couple of hours, Hefner and Chuck went on that way, rapping about sex with animals and anything else you might imagine. They both seemed excited. In fact, they reminded me of two kids talking about what they had just gotten for Christmas.

I may not have said much but I know what I was thinking. Until that night, I had felt that Chuck was absolutely insane, far gone. I was sure there would be no one else like him in the whole world. And then we meet someone very rich and famous like Hugh Hefner, a very well-known name around the world, and in an instant he is right down there on the same level with Chuck Traynor. That really bothered me.

If you met the two of them, you would think they'd have nothing in common. And I'm sure that Hugh Hefner would never send a girl into a store and ask her to do something with a salesman. Nor can I imagine Hefner doing the kind of thing to me that Chuck routinely did. Although the styles were different, they did have a lot in common. And that first night, as they got to know each other, they were talking about every kind of kinky sex. Okay, they didn't look the same and they didn't act the same, but they both lived on the same street.

After that night, Chuck and I became part of the "family." That meant that we were given special golden cards. Most people driving up to the gate of the Playboy Mansion West need an invitation or their names must be on a special list. People with golden cards come and go as they like.

In very short order, we became special members of the family. I'm not so sure that this was all a result of our own natural charm: I think it may have had something to do with the fact that we had a dog named Rufus. Whatever the reason, the dog also became a member of Hefner's official family. Not only did the publisher arrange for the dog to be shipped in from Florida, he then set him up in the lap of luxury. That's right, the Playboy Mansion West kennel. I can only imagine the dog's confusion as the Playboy limousine picked him up at the airport and drove him to his new five-acre estate.

While Rufus was living it up in the kennels, Chuck and I had been given the run of the Mansion. We were practically living there. We had joined the rest of the freeloaders for the movies, the food, the parties and the regular Wednesday night orgies. On orgy night, which is what everyone called it, the regulars would sit through a pornographic movie—*Deep Throat* was shown several times—and then join the others in the pool, the Jacuzzi or anywhere else that sexual pleasure might be available.

Not always was orgy night announced in advance. It might start off as a regular evening—music, backgammon, socializing—and then the word would come down: "Tonight is orgy night."

Most people seem to feel that the Playboy mansion is always loaded with bunnies, centerfold girls, and famous actors. But whenever orgy night was announced, the real celebrities had the basic good sense to get out while the getting was good. As did most of the young women who wanted to maintain their amateur status.

Some of the girls who did stay for orgy night told me they were hired to be there. They called themselves "models," not hookers, but they weren't being paid to have their pictures taken. They were joined by some weirdo women and young thrill-seekers who were probably there on the chance of meeting a real live movie star. One of the regulars at these orgies, and a favorite at the mansion, was a girl who didn't look any older than seventeen, Lila. Lila was always invited, and she just had to say the word to have the limousine sent to her home.

Many of the male orgy-goers were family. Often they were people who were almost celebrities or people who worked for celebrities. Actors who had never gone from television to movies; a hair dresser who worked for the stars; a real estate man who specialized in Beverly Hills; an agent; the owner of a famous restaurant. It may have been called orgy night but I thought of it as flunky night.

There was no doubt that Hefner was the head of the household but he never seemed to be truly a part of his "family." I always got the feeling that he was a very lonely man. Even when he was in the middle of a crowd, laughing and talking, he seemed to be holding onto his pipe for dear life.

It was as if he curtained off part of himself from the crowd. The more I got to know him, the more unhappy he seemed. He is used constantly. Nobody around him seems to care for Hugh Hefner, the person; they're all there for the lobster and the caviar and the sight of celebrities.

Sometimes he reminded me of King Midas. He had designed this perfect palace, and he had all these perfect looking people around him, all the sensational music and all the best games, the finest food and drink, and, yet, he could really touch none of it—and none of it could touch him.

Other times he reminded me of that movie, *The Great Gatsby*. Some of the family would stop off on their way to work, buzz for a butler, have some breakfast, then be on their way. These people never brought anything to the Mansion except their bodies. You'd never see anyone bring a bottle of booze or a gift. Oh, no, they'd come to Hefner's house, eat his food, drink his booze, watch his movie, pick up the chicks he provided; then they'd go home. Most often, they'd never even see their host.

Once, about three o'clock in the morning, when most of us were packing up to go home, Joanie, Hefner's secretary, came running down the stairs in a panic. She was really schizing out because Hefner had decided to come down and join the party just as everyone else was leaving.

"Oh, will you please stay?" she asked one person. And: "Please, would you mind staying for a while?" And: "Hef will be coming down soon and we should have someone here when he comes down." And: "Please stay, I think Hef will want to play backgammon. Oh, please stay."

That whole scene was so sad. Everyone who had been leaving froze and then went back to what they had been doing. When Hefner appeared, wearing pajamas and a bathrobe, holding a Pepsi in his hand, he was greeted by waves of false hilarity, as though the party was still going full blast. There were the smiles and the laughs and the big hellos. And I guess, when all was said and done, that was the price people paid for his hospitality.

And Hefner's hospitality was impressive, especially to members of the family. The *Playboy* publisher would decide to fly to his Chicago headquarters and many of us just got on his private jet with him and took the trip. If Hefner was staying in Chicago for a couple of weeks, we'd check in with him at the Chicago mansion. Quite a few of the girls who surrounded him seemed able to commute from one mansion to the other.

Coming into the Chicago mansion, Hefner was greeted by a girl named Karen. She struck me as typical of the women in his life. She was a tall, blonde, gorgeous Texan; I was struck by how dazzling she was. Early the next morning a woman said hello to me in the hallway and when I gave her a blank look, she said, "I'm Karen—we met yesterday." I gave her a second look and had trouble believing it was the same person. She wasn't wearing makeup and she hadn't yet put on her wig. Or her glamorous clothes. The best parts of her—and this was typical of the women in Hefner's life—could be stored in boxes. They were gorgeous, as long as you didn't look at them too closely. Then you became aware of the plastic; they reminded me of dolls that you dressed up and played with.

Hefner's bedroom in the Chicago mansion was chaotic. He had a videotape machine set up beside the bed so that he could make tapes of himself in bed. There were spools of eight-millimeter film lying around. And stacks of pages everywhere, the raw material from an upcoming issue of the magazine.

A different kind of person—more intellectual, I guess—seemed to hang around the Chicago mansion. The California crowd was louder, brasher, more free wheeling. In Chicago they were more formal, more uptight. Some of them didn't even know who I was.

Despite this, Chuck was right at home in the Chicago mansion. He soon discovered that this was where Hefner kept his library of eight-millimeter movies. Each morning during our stay there, Chuck would check out dozens of these films. He made me sit for hours at a time, up to eight hours in a single stretch, watching people have sex with each other, with animals, with whatever else was handy. Chuck couldn't get enough of that.

What I remember most about the Chicago mansion was a cook named George; he made a Beef Wellington that was not to be believed.

While we were in Chicago, I became aware of a new kind of business possibility, one that wouldn't require me to do things I didn't want to do. While there, for example, I met the writer-cartoonist Shel Silverstein and we talked about doing an album of country-and-western songs together. Although Chuck managed to botch that deal, it set me to thinking.

Suddenly we were jetting all over the country. From Los Angeles to Chicago to New York to Florida to Nashville and back to Los Angeles again. This was all part of ending our life in Florida and starting over again in California.

We stopped long enough in New York to make the second movie, *Deep Throat, Part II*. I still don't understand what that movie was about but I can tell you how it was explained to me. The central figure is a computer working for the CIA and the FBI: The computer is tired of government work and wants to make spaghetti. In the course of the movie, the computer makes love to me. Maybe you can understand why it was never released or, if it was released, why you've never heard of it.

Bad as that movie was, it taught me some of the rewards of being a celebrity. They were so anxious to see my name on the billboards that it didn't much matter what I did in the movie. The result: I didn't have to do any of the sexual acrobatics that made the first movie such a success. The producers decided that the people who had enjoyed the first film would buy tickets for this one, no matter what was in it.

During the filming of *Deep Throat, Part II*, I became friendly with one of my co-stars, Andrea True. Andrea True was very intelligent, a college graduate, and much too smart to be doing what she did for a living. During the making of the film, she got all of the porno actors together and organized them into a union. It might seem silly, but they really needed a union. For most of them, an eight-hour day was a big step up.

One night Chuck invited Andrea over to our hotel room and a scene came down with the three of us; she was into that kind of thing. It was then that she told us she also had her own little business going on the side, and one of her customers was a top executive with a publishing house. He wanted to meet me to talk about a book.

So one evening after we were through shooting, Andrea took us over to the offices of Pinnacle Books in New York. There we met Andrea's friend, David Zentner. He and Chuck talked for a while and then shook hands on a deal that would

give Chuck a large advance—I think it was $40,000—as well
as a writer who would do all the actual work.

With all the money coming in and a future that seemed
promising, Chuck was confused. It no longer made any sense
for me to be a hooker. In fact, that kind of thing might just
damage my value as a movie star-celebrity-author-godknows-
what.

And this was my first payoff; I had turned my last trick.
Oh, Chuck would still tell me what to do and whom to do it
with—if he snapped his fingers, I did it—but no longer was
he renting my body to the man who drove the soda truck or
a manufacturer of farm tools. The payoff would not be twenty
or thirty or forty dollars; it would be more power or weird
sex or nearness to fame or, sometimes, all of these.

Now I was beginning to see a new escape route. The more
well known I became, the more other people came into my
life, the less control Chuck would have over me.

# *seventeen*

The money was now streaming in to Chuck, and the source of the stream seemed to be California. We had settled down in a rented beach cottage at Malibu and Chuck had bought a Jaguar. The next thing Chuck did was arrange for our second home, our home away from home, the Playboy Mansion West.

Chuck's primary goal was to bring Hugh Hefner and myself together sexually. He saw this as the beginning of a great palship. Chuck had this picture of Hefner and himself as arm-in-arm buddies, sharing the sexual wealth of the world, dividing up playmates and bunnies equally. Of course, that never came down. All that did come down were a couple of scenes with Hefner.

Before going down to the pool, Chuck gave me a briefing. It would be all right if I got involved with another woman or with Hefner himself, but if any other man came near me, I was to discourage his advances. Chuck would be right there if I needed help.

The first time we went to orgy night, Hefner didn't show up. As soon as he realized the publisher was not going to make an appearance, Chuck whisked me away. The follow-

ing Wednesday we waited again, and this time Hefner came
down to the Jacuzzi. As soon as he took off his bathrobe and
stepped out into the water, Chuck started pushing me toward
him.

Hefner seemed in a playful mood. He was into frolicking
around, going from one girl to another like a bee buzzing
flowers. He carried a huge bottle of Johnson's baby oil with
him and he was rubbing everyone down with the oil. There
were about twelve people in the Jacuzzi and, before long,
they were all coated with oil. It got all through my hair and
I thought it was a real nuisance.

I could tell that Hefner had mixed feelings about me. He
definitely wanted me there in the Jacuzzi but he didn't seem
to want anything to come down between the two of us. I
think many men had trouble with the fact that I was the star
of *Deep Throat*; they saw the size of the men in the movie
and that tended to make them self-conscious. I would say
that Hefner felt a definite inhibition.

At any rate, he was in no rush to get to me. He seemed
to enjoy moseying around with the other females. Meanwhile,
Chuck was afraid that some other male would latch onto me
first and he kept pushing me over toward Hefner. Hefner
couldn't ignore it any longer, so he tried to direct me over
toward the young girl who was a regular at the mansion.

"Why don't you go over to Lila?" he said.

Lila needed no urging. She loved to be the center of
attention. I still don't know how old she was, but she looked
like a high school girl. So Lila and I got together and put on
a little show for the publisher.

Chuck wouldn't take part in an orgy himself, not as a rule.
His whole aim was to bring Hefner and myself together. The
reason Chuck wouldn't take part was that he had sexual
problems and he didn't want them revealed. He was naked
in the water but if a girl came over to him and tried to get
something started, there'd be no reaction.

What happened was really not my cup of tea. While Lila

and I were together, the rest of the orgy-goers stopped what they were doing and formed a circle around us so that they could get a closer look at what was happening. It reminded me of those old Fred Astaire movies where all the other dancers suddenly stopped what they were doing and formed a circle around Fred and Ginger. And then the bystanders started making comments.

For some strange reason, the action was not enough—the audience also wanted sound effects. It was all very humiliating, another embarrassment in an endless string of embarrassments, but the orgy must go on.

Even Chuck contributed his talents to the show. He decided to demonstrate a new trick he had been practicing; this involved putting his entire fist into my body. One of the other men held my body out of the water while Chuck was doing that to me. Then Lila took over for Chuck, doing the same thing with her fist. At this point, everyone there applauded, again just like in one of those old Fred Astaire movies.

Hefner finally got himself aroused enough to approach me. I think he realized that Chuck would give him no peace unless he did something, so he came up behind me and entered me in the backside. That was his big thrill and chill and that was that. When he finished, Hefner disappeared and Chuck and I left soon after that.

I'm not sure what the others at the orgy that night were doing. I didn't bother looking around much. I'm still that kind of a person—if two people are making love, I look the other way.

That night Chuck was very pleased, very up. I had finally done something right. Now it was inevitable, now he and Hefner would be good buddies and pals. After all, Hef—good old buddy, Hef—had used his woman, hadn't he? Chuck could hardly wait for the next favor he was going to do for his pal, Hef. He was going to show the publisher something he had always wanted to see: He was going to show him a real live woman making love to a real live dog.

I was glad that the dog was going to be Rufus. I had been able to discourage him in the past, and I felt sure I'd be able to discourage him now.

The night I was supposed to do it, Chuck was very edgy. He was on my case all night long.

"Listen, Babe," he said. "You better make sure it works out tonight. I told Hef that it'd be no sweat."

"I don't know," I said. "Rufus doesn't seem to want to."

"Well, tonight, he *better* want to," he said. "Neither one of you better fuck this up tonight or you're both gonna wind up in the pound tomorow."

"All I know is—"

"And all I know is it better fucking work out. If it doesn't happen right away, just hang in there. Stay with it this time. Tell Hef he shouldn't be too impatient, it takes time to make it work."

The scene was set to come down late that night, after a movie and after most of the other guests had gone home. Hefner called Security and told them to post guards at the bathhouse. One of the guards brought Rufus over from the kennel and then he joined a second guard stationed outside the bathhouse.

When we went over there, Hefner was dressed casually, pajamas and bathrobe. Chuck sat down on a large pillow but the publisher remained standing as he talked about "the excitement of this moment."

Hefner had no way of knowing I was there against my will, no way of realizing that I was Chuck's prisoner. I know I shouldn't hold something like this against him, but it was being staged for his benefit—and he was a part of it all. Months later, when a mutual friend told him that Chuck had forced me to do everything I did, he was very upset by it.

"Okay, Linda," Chuck said. "Take off your clothes."

I did everything Chuck told me to do. I stripped down and bent over on a carpeted section of the floor and waited for Rufus to come over. When the dog set about positioning himself, that was the moment for me to move. It didn't take much movement. What I did was just back ever so slightly against the dog. The instant I did that, Rufus backed off.

Nothing happened. And I knew all the time that nothing was going to happen. I did it one time because I had to, because they had a gun. But this time there were no guns. And I would rather take the worst beating in the world than ever let it happen again. So I made sure that nothing happened.

Hefner was very understanding.

"You know," he said, "Lila's been having the same problem. We can't figure it."

"Just give her some time," Chuck said. "Linda can work this thing out."

Chuck was trying desperately to salvage something for his pal, Hef, but nothing was going to work. Rufus kept backing away.

"This is really odd," Hefner said, "it's just this way with Lila. You have to wonder why it keeps happening."

I could have told him why. Instead I tried to muster up an air of disappointment to match his own.

"Well," he said, finally, "these things happen."

As we went home that night, I was feeling triumphant. I had managed to eliminate one of the worst threats in my life. And, once again, I had enjoyed a small victory over Chuck Traynor. I think, however, he was beginning to be suspicious. Throughout the ride home that night, he was moody and sullen. Just before we got out of the car, he turned on me.

"It was all your fault!"

Who, me? Of course, he was right. But he won't know that for sure until he reads these words.

# *eighteen*

And so I became a best-selling author. The way you become a best-selling author is this: Every night for two weeks you get a list of questions to answer; Chuck Traynor tells you how to answer these questions and you give those answers to a tape recorder; then a professional writer types it, arranges it, spells it right, and calls it *Inside Linda Lovelace*. The publisher adds a centerfold and a bunch of other near-naked pictures and then you have a best-selling book.

What happened during the writing of this book, and the next one written under my name, makes me doubt every book I read. Sometimes I wonder if the publisher of this book will find a way to change this story around. Of course this time I'm not being introduced to a publisher by a call girl, and this time I believe there will not be any naked centerfold pictures.

The only honesty in that first book was the accidental honesty of its dedication: "To Chuck Traynor—the creator."

That's certainly accurate enough, slightly more accurate than the message of the book, a message that was set down very clearly in the opening chapter: *I live for sex, will never get enough of it, and will continue to try every day to tune my physical mechanism to finer and finer perfection.*

The book is a pack of lies. My "thoughts" about mastur-bation: *Then, at age twelve, and now at age twenty-two, I'm an incorrigible masturbator*. And on teenage lesbianism: *I saw her naked body and tried not to show my interest, but you already know about me; I'm not exactly turned off by the female anatomy*. And about losing my virginity to the awesome Chuck Traynor: *The fat rocklike muscle tore into me like a battering ram, and I nearly fainted from the shock . . . I came in seconds*.

If it wasn't so awful I might laugh. I see that Chuck Traynor is described repeatedly as the world's greatest lover. And I was his good student: *He didn't bullwhip me into per-forming like a circus pony. I was the most willing pupil a teacher could ever have. Since I was so earnest, he devoted the time necessary to help me with my accomplishments*.

Reading the book now, I see Chuck's fear that the truth would one day surface. Here are my feelings about *Deep Throat*: *If I didn't love what I did, no money on earth could make me do it. Like my work? Friends, I love every second of it . . . on and off camera*. In a chapter about Michelle's party: *I'll admit I got a little excited by the bizarre carry-ings-on*. The reason I exposed myself in public: *I'm a com-pulsive flasher, if you know what that is*. And even an ex-planation of the horrible bruises on my body in *Deep Throat*: *Would you believe it that the day before we started shooting, I bumped against a stupid bedpost and ended up with a bruise on my hip that looked like I'd been in a scrimmage with the Los Angeles Rams*.

The book should have been called *Inside Chuck Traynor*. Even the sexual incidents they thought up for me—for ex-ample, making love to a mother-daughter combination—were things that had happened to Chuck. And, of course, the philosophy was pure Chuck: *We should worry more about real issues and less about what a few uptight fogeys think are issues. If this country is free, shouldn't each person be given a choice to live as he wishes*.

I hate the thought that people today can still pick up that

piece of trash and think it has anything to do with me or with my life. Which is why I'm so delighted that Chuck Traynor, in a 1976 interview with Leonard Lyons, told the truth: "I wrote the book *Inside Linda Lovelace* with another guy before Linda and I split up. I created all the sex situations in it just as I created Linda Lovelace."

Now that we were branching out in so many directions, Chuck decided that we needed an office on Sunset Boulevard, the home office of Linda Lovelace Enterprises. Chuck put together the companies with the assistance of lawyer Phil Mandina. Anyway, now that we had a company and an office, we needed someone who knew how to type. Chuck mentioned this to Hugh Hefner one night.

"We've got to find a secretary," he said.

"What kind of qualifications are you looking for?" Hefner asked.

"She should have big tits."

"I think I know someone."

The woman we hired, Dolores, was a former secretary of Hefner's. She had been a starlet in those beach-blanket movies and more than met Chuck's specifications. Dolores was also a Hollywood fixture and knew everyone there was to know in the entertainment world. On top of all this, Dolores proved to be a good friend to me and a source of strength when I needed strength most.

Although we continued to visit Hefner's home, Chuck began to realize that the publisher was never going to be one of his pals, never going to share his wealth with him. And there had to be more to life than backgammon. It seemed a good time to accept an invitation from Sammy Davis Jr.

As we went to Sammy's house that first night, Chuck went through the regular celebrity briefing. I was to lay down every hint I could think of and if anyone else hinted at anything, I was to pick up on it right away.

"If Sammy suggests anything—I mean anything at all— you just go along with it one-hundred percent."

Our first night at Sammy's house was a typical Hollywood

social evening, dinner followed by a movie in the star's private screening room. And then the four of us—Chuck and myself, Sammy and Altovise—sat around and talked. That night the conversation remained fairly general despite Chuck's constant efforts to divert it into the gutter. Once, when Chuck was doing this, Sammy indicated surprise.

"Oh? Are you two into scenes?" he said.

To me, a "scene" was a sexual happening—an orgy, or a swap or practically anything outside the norm.

"We're into anything at all," Chuck said.

"Yeah?" Sammy seemed thoughtful. "Well, I can dig that."

Then we let it slide. I can no longer remember the first time that a scene actually came down between Sammy and myself but once it did happen, it happened almost every night. Sammy would start a movie going in the screening room and then he and I would wander off to another part of the house, leaving Chuck and Altovise together.

It wasn't all scenes with Sammy. Every night we were together, we'd spend hours just talking and sometimes we'd spend the whole night just rapping about his past. Sammy loved to remember his days as a child performer, part of a group that featured his father and his uncle. He told me about traveling arcoss the country in those days and what would happen when their old car broke down. He talked about his marriages and kids. And he particularly loved talking about his songs. He'd play tapes of himself singing as a youngster and as a star. "Hey, listen to this," he'd say, "you'll see how my voice has changed."

Sammy never asked me much about my past, about my growing up, but that would have seemed as ordinary to him as it does to me. He was interested in now, in what I was doing with my career at the moment. For a time he seemed intrigued by the thought of my becoming part of his show, but that never came about. He did suggest that I put together a big Las Vegas act. He had advice for every part of my career except movies; he knew he wasn't the world's greatest movie actor and he wasn't getting many film roles.

Sammy looked like a savior to me. Just being in his company kept me out of other situations. And I liked him as a person. He wasn't constantly molesting me and I enjoyed just being with him, listening to his music and his words.

There were scenes with Sammy, but he wasn't beating me or hurting me. He had his own code of marital fidelity—he explained to me that he could do anything except have normal intercourse because that, the act of making love, would be cheating on his wife. What he wanted me to do, then, was to deep-throat him. Because that would not be an act of infidelity.

Chuck and Sammy seemed to have an understanding with each other. Whenever Sammy led me away for the evening, Chuck never said a word or came looking for us. This was because Chuck was sure that Sammy would do what Hefner had never done, fix him up with a lot of far-out chicks. It would have been easy for Sammy to keep Chuck happy. He would have just had to say that he was going to introduce him to a chick who liked to be whipped until she bled. If you told Chuck something like that—and you could promise it at some indefinite date—he'd do anything for you. However, Sammy never did make that effort.

While there were scenes between Chuck and Altovise, she couldn't stand Chuck. According to Sammy, Altovise despised Chuck and wanted her husband to find someone else for her.

To this day, I have trouble understanding Altovise. If you've ever seen her, you know what a truly beautiful woman she is. And while all this was going on around her, she remained silent. She never really participated in the conversation. She was just there. I could see that Altovise wasn't into scenes any more than I was. She went along with it because it was what Sammy wanted.

I always felt a kinship with Altovise. We were alike in

many ways but not alike in motivation. She did things to keep her man happy; I did things to keep my man from killing me. More than once Sammy said that he thought Altovise and I were the same kind of person; we were both "beautiful people." The one big difference, as he saw it, was that Altovise wasn't super-freaky and I was. He said that she would go along with things but she never really got into it. I, on the other hand, was really into it.

Why didn't I tell Sammy the truth? Because there was another side to him. When he was talking with me he would often describe things that he wanted to do to me. He would like to tie me down on a bed, then have other women come in and make love to me while he watched. That other side of Sammy could be scary. But even when talking about it, he would speak in a gentle voice and he never actually did anything. But I always wondered. And I was afraid that if he found out the truth, that I was not a super-freak then he'd have no more to do with me and I'd be back with Chuck all the time.

Only occasionally did Sammy's far-out ideas become reality. There were times when the two men had Altovise and myself go through a "scene" together while they watched. But I'm as sure now, as I was then, that they were the only two in the room to get any pleasure from that at all.

The four of us were always together. Every night, most of the night. And when Sammy felt like a little golfing vacation in Hawaii, we all packed up and went along. When Sammy got a suite at the Kahala Hilton, we just moved in.

During our stay in Hawaii, a change came over Sammy. One night at a private party, he and I were talking together and he said that his feelings about me were getting serious. He said that he had fought it but it was no use; he was falling in love and he wanted me with him the rest of his life. Altovise happened to overhear some of this and, naturally, she was hurt and angry. Sammy tried to calm her down but she left the party.

"She's gone back to the hotel," he said.

"I'm sorry, Sammy—you should be with her."

"No," he said. "I'm right where I should be, right where I want to be."

After that, things became even more intense. In a way, I was using him; he was the only one on earth who could prevent Chuck from doing what he wanted to do to me. But Sammy was a romantic man and the word "love" came into our conversations more and more often.

One night we were going to a nightclub opening and I decided to dress all in white: a white gown and a white fox wrap that a shop in Beverly Hills let me borrow for the evening. Sammy took one look at me, then dashed upstairs. When he came down, he was also dressed in white—a white tuxedo, white top hat, and white gloves.

He was always making romantic gestures. He put me on a pedestal and he bought me gifts, a gold bracelet, one of the early Polaroid cameras, and many trinkets. I always wondered how Altovise reacted when he catered to me. Or how she reacted when we all were out in public—Sammy and I would be creating a stir, signing autographs, while Chuck and Altovise remained in the background.

Often Sammy would talk about marriage but it was strictly what-if talk. What if I left Chuck and what if he left Altovise and what if we decided to get married and what if. . . . I didn't want him to divorce anyone to marry me. Because I didn't see where my life would get any better. What was happening between us wasn't all that terrific. All that was happening, really, was that he was keeping me out of worse scenes, away from sadism and freakishness.

Sammy Davis Jr. gave me many gifts but the biggest present of all was one moment of revenge. I sense that this will not sound like much revenge to any reader who is aware of all that Chuck did to me. However, it was the only time I saw Chuck get a taste of his own medicine.

On this particular night Altovise had managed to find something else to do. The three of us—Chuck, Sammy, myself—were in the screening room watching a porno movie.

Or, rather, the two men were watching the movie. I was on my knees in front of Sammy, deep-throating him while he watched the movie.

"I really dig that," Sammy was whispering. "I'd like to know how you do it. When are you going to teach me? When're you going to show me how you do that?"

Sammy often talked like that, asking me when I was going to teach him how to deep-throat someone. Sometimes I thought he was just joking and sometimes I wasn't so sure. On this particular night, Sammy suddenly looked over at Chuck sitting a few seats away. Chuck was staring at the movie screen.

"Hey, you think Chuck would mind?"

"Mind?" I whispered back. "No, that's the kind of thing he'd go for in a big way. But let me set it up for you."

Of course, this was definitely *not* the kind of ·thing Chuck would go for in a big way. In fact, that may have been his greatest fear, the one possibility he dreaded most. Whenever he was going to put down another man, he would call him "that fag."

A psychiatrist could probably explain this. All I have are suspicions. Chuck existed in a very narrow sexual area. Probably because of his experiences with his mother, he hated all women and could never just have straight sex with a woman. But he was also a former Marine and a gun nut; in that super-macho world, there was no room for gays. So where did that leave him? That left him with cruelty and animals and whatever other bizarre possibility he could dream up.

The room was pitch black except for a flickering light bouncing off a movie screen. Since Chuck was only a couple of feet away from us, he knew full well what I had just done with Sammy. He didn't move at all—his eyes never left the movie screen—as I went over to him and reached out to unzip his trousers.

"Hey, you can't just sit there and watch," I said to Chuck. "You can't just sit there."

As I was talking to Chuck, I signaled for Sammy to come on over. Chuck grunted at me and shifted his weight, making it easier for me to do the job. He must have been really into the dirty movie because he didn't realize what was happening until it happened. I was the one who unzipped his trousers, but I wasn't the one who knelt in front of him.

A minute or two went by before Chuck realized that something was different. Then, although Chuck didn't utter a sound, his eyes were screaming for help. He looked back at me, boiling mad now, and with his right hand gestured for me to come over and free him.

I just shrugged my shoulders and laughed. Perhaps this won't seem like much revenge to the reader, but, finally, after all the awful things Chuck had done to me, I was able to put him through an ordeal, a sexual ordeal at that. You may not think he was suffering much. But that's only because you weren't there to see the agony on his face.

I was sure that Chuck would say something and end the little experiment but he didn't say a word. That was so typical. He had such unnatural respect for anyone in a position of power that he didn't dare complain. He let the scene go on and on without interrupting it.

Each time that Sammy showed signs of slowing down, I kept him going with instructional encouragement. It was, ironically enough, the same instruction that Chuck had once given me.

"No, no, Sammy," I said, "push down a little more—he'll like that. Yeah, that's right. Keep going. You're doing fine."

Chuck was glaring at me but he didn't utter a word. He would put up with anything rather than risk losing the friendship of Sammy Davis, Jr. He would rather have a heart attack than say no to a celebrity. The fact that Chuck was not responding didn't seem to bother Sammy.

"Not so fast," I said. "It's better when you do it nice and slowly. That's right, slow it down . . . yes, that's right, that's very good."

In time, Sammy finally gave up on Chuck. I knew that

I'd be punished, but this time it was worth it. The expression on Chuck's face that night will be with me always.

The experience revealed something about Chuck that I hadn't known. His cowardice. There he was, in pain and scared, but unable to speak up. He didn't know how to handle it, didn't know what to do. He expected *me* to save *him*. And this was really nothing at all, nothing at all compared to the things he made me do. And he couldn't handle that. He couldn't handle the littlest thing. It was really nothing and he flipped out!

My time with Sammy was almost at an end. One night soon after, to my great surprise, he wanted normal sex with me. It was the first time we ever had intercourse; the first time he ever made love to me. In effect, he was choosing me over Altovise. However, the first time we ever made love was also the last time. In a few days I would be free of Chuck and that whole way of life would be behind me.

# *nineteen*

Living in Hollywood, you begin to forget that outside there is still a normal world with normal people. California is the land of the super-freaks and they all seem to come to Hollywood sooner or later. And when they were in Hollywood, they looked us up.

That's why Chuck loved California. It was easy for him to find people as sick as himself. Remembering the kind of people he'd bring home still grosses me out.

Just one example, no more. But one example should be enough.

One day Chuck had a photographer taking pictures of me and the photographer showed Chuck some other pictures he had recently taken. Pictures of a blonde with empty eyes and a full chest.

"Yeah," Chuck decided, "she looks like a freaky chick. What's her phone number?"

The photographer looked up the girl's telephone number in his appointment book. He said that her name was Brigit. While we were still there talking, Chuck picked up the phone and dialed her number. He introduced himself as Linda Lovelace's manager and said that he had just been admiring her photographs.

"Nice body, honey," he said. "I've got a feeling we may be able to help you out. Why don't you come down here right now?"

Within ten minutes, Brigit was there. And Chuck had it right; she was a freak. I don't know how someone can tell that by just looking at a photograph but Chuck had an instinct. The two of them talked for just a few minutes and the next thing I knew, we were all on our way home together. Brigit told us that she was just starting out as a model. Later she would be featured in many girlie magazines and even a pornographic movie or two, but then she was unknown.

For once, Chuck didn't have to push a thing. As soon as the car was moving toward home, I felt a hand on my thigh. Glancing down, I saw that Brigit had one hand on me and the other hand on Chuck. Besides being ambidextrous, she was a non-stop talker. She was just *thrilled* to meet me; she was just *crazy* about dildoes; her *special* favorite was giving and receiving enemas.

"Oh yeah?" That interested Chuck. "Far out!"

Once we got home, Brigit was all over me. The more I looked at her, the more I saw Chuck. She was a strange mirror image of him, a woman as perverted as he was. Chuck supplied the dildoes and she supplied the imagination. For a long time, Chuck contented himself with watching her work on me. And then—it must have been four o'clock in the morning—she had a suggestion for him.

"If you've got a douche bag," she said, "I really feel like an enema."

"We've got a douche bag," Chuck said.

"Wow, I'm really sleepy," I said. "I've just got to get some sleep."

"You just stay there," Chuck said. "I want you to watch this."

Well, watching was better than doing. And so, while I became the observer, Chuck became a participant. What happened next was enough to make me feel physically sick, but I didn't dare leave the bathroom.

The scene came down in the bathtub. Chuck was lying down flat in the bathtub and Brigit was squatting over him. She bent over so that he could give her an enema. She kept it in her as long as she could and even then she was saying, "More, more!" When it was impossible for her to take any more, she squatted directly over his face. He pulled out the plug and the stuff was all over his face and his shoulders. Then she sat down in that mess. The next thing, Chuck was taking his fingers and rubbing it through the stuff and then he was wiping it over her face and into her mouth. It was all I could do to keep from throwing up. They were so wrapped up in what was coming down, they forgot all about me.

Okay, that was Brigit. And to me, that will always be California.

I have to admit that California was also the land of opportunity. If the people were easy, so was the money. Sometimes it looked to me as though people were trying to force money on Chuck.

We were there for just a few weeks and Chuck found himself working on a dozen different deals. Head Shampoo was talking about my doing commercials; another guy was printing posters; someone wanted to back a Las Vegas act; there was talk of record albums, movies, books, you name it.

Not that the money ever became part of my life. Whatever money came in went right to Chuck and his bank accounts. If I needed money, say, to have a tooth fixed, he'd delay it as long as he could. First he'd have to see if I was covered by any insurance; then he'd want to know whether it was something that really had to be fixed; and then maybe —just maybe—he'd have it fixed legitimately. Trying to get Chuck to part with my money was never easy.

And whenever an offer came up that genuinely interested

me, Chuck managed to ruin it. The country-and-western album was just the first of many busted balloons. One deal
that really excited me was a movie that Buck Henry wanted
to make with Milos Forman. They wanted me to star in it.
This would have been legitimate, quality, the big time. Even
Chuck was impressed. In fact, Chuck was so impressed that
he made the two film-makers a counter offer.

"If you guys really want to make a movie with Linda,"
he said, "then you could have her for a week."

That took care of that little deal. I didn't know much
about Buck Henry or Milos Forman then, but I could tell
they were serious people. I also knew that I could be in
any movie they might make without embarrassment. When
the deals did fall through, it was generally because Chuck
did not know how to operate in the straight world. He
never realized that someone somewhere might do something
without expecting a sexual payoff.

Although I was terribly let down after that, there was
one good side to the experience. The more that decent
people became interested in me for decent reasons, the
stronger I became.

Every other day, Chuck had new papers for me to sign.
Releases, deals, contracts that tied me to him forever.
Everything that was put in front of me I signed. There was
only one small moment of rebellion. We once flew from
California to Florida to meet with Philip Mandina and sign
papers forming one corporation or another. As they piled
up the papers for me to sign, I thought I'd throw a scare
into them.

"I don't think I should sign anything until I show it to
my lawyer."

The bottom fell out of Mandina's face and Chuck spun
toward me.

"What's this about a lawyer?" he said. "What's this fucking talk about a fucking lawyer?"

"Come on, Linda," Mandina said. "Be smart. You know
you're going to do what your husband tells you to do."

My little ploy had gotten a large reaction. But the experience didn't tell me anything I didn't already know. These two men had raped me every way it was possible for one human being to rape another. And never, at any time, had either one of them considered my interests in anything.

I've still got the contract for employment that I signed that day. Right below my signature is Chuck's signature. And there's a salary clause that grants me 3 percent of my gross earnings. The contract is for ten years and was renewable for another ten years beyond that. No wonder they were frightened that I might have another lawyer look at it.

That summer of 1973, Chuck decided that I should star in a musical review. He had found a backer, a Gerry Brodsky, and he was willing to put up a mountain of cash. He found a theater in Miami that wanted me. He had gotten calls from Las Vegas. And now, using Brodsky's money, we were going to interview producers who knew how to put together a musical stage show.

Introducing: David Winters. David Winters was well known as both a choreographer and a producer. He had been in *West Side Story*, had worked on Elvis Presley movies, and had put together successful musical acts for Ann-Margret, Raquel Welch and many others.

All I knew about David Winters was that he had a reputation for extravagance. I was told that if the budget was $20,000, he would manage to bring in a show for $60,000. But he also had a reputation for bringing in nothing but winners.

Describing David Winters as flamboyant is to seriously understate the case. He habitually wore stretch pants and boots, a loose chemise with puffed sleeves, and a pocketbook with jingling little bells on it. As I met David Winters for the first time, he handed me a single long-stemmed rose.

I took one look at David Winters and decided he was wonderful. Chuck took one look at David Winters and decided he was "a fag."

We both decided to hire him. And David immediately assembled a team that had worked with him before, the best talent money could buy. Voice and dance coaches, a back-up team of dancers and singers, a choreographer named Joe Cassini, and a writer, Mel Mandel.

On August twenty-first we signed contracts to open at Miami's Paramount Theater on November first. The salary was to be $15,000 a week for two weeks. Three twenty-minute shows a day. There was only one bad clause in the contract, this one inked in: "Lovelace agrees to appear nude at a point in time during the act." Chuck signed it and I signed it and it was co-signed and guaranteed by a certain Philip Mandina, Esq.

It wasn't a perfect contract. So Susan Hayward never had to sign a contract calling for her "to appear nude at a point in time during her act." At least I was going to be doing honest work. And it *was* work. I started immediately working with the vocal coaches where our first problem was trying to find out what my key was. And then trying to find songs I could sing. We had to begin by agreeing that I wasn't an Ella Fitzgerald or a Judy Garland; I had a range that could most politely be described as limited. But I could carry a tune. Some tunes anyway.

Actually, I *love* music—I've always loved music and I still love it today. It's my favorite escape. If someone turns on a radio, my feet want to dance. Just listening to music gives me a feeling of well being. When Chuck realized that, it became one of his favorite punishments; he would forbid me to listen to music. And now, for the first time, music itself became an important part of my whole life.

At the same time I was learning how to sing, I was practicing dancing. And, also at the same time, I was going over the comedy routines that Mel Mandel was writing for me. The script was a collection of double-entendres joined together by this comic theme: Being Linda Lovelace is not easy; in fact, it's hard to make even casual conversation.

The opening went something like this: "Good evening,

ladies and gentlemen, thank you for *coming* . . . Oh, excuse me, I can't say that. It's so *hard* . . . oops . . . it's so difficult for me to say anything. Every time I open my mouth . . . oops, sorry about that." It was a little crude, but it was also a little cute. If I'd been in the audience, I might have giggled at some of the lines.

Once the rehearsals started, I began to feel good, really good. I never worked harder in my life, but it was decent work. Singing and dancing and learning new things. And somehow, the more I did, the more I was able to do. And the less important Chuck seemed.

Chuck must have seen the danger here. Although he didn't say anything to me, he seemed to be doing everything possible to undermine the production. At this time he was into partying in a big way, staying out until four o'clock every morning, sleeping until noon. The only trouble was that my rehearsals were supposed to begin at nine in the morning.

This was one of the few times in my life I found the courage to speak up to him.

"Chuck, this is just no good. I've got to get to my rehearsals on time. If I'm going to get up on a stage and sing and dance, I don't want to make a fool of myself. I've got to know what I'm supposed to do."

"Hey, Babe, take it easy there."

"This just makes basic sense," I said. "We're renting the rehearsal space. We've hired all these people to teach me and—"

"Who the fuck do you think you're talking to?" he said. "Just who the fuck do you think you are?"

After that, Chuck had me missing one appointment after another. If my singing lesson was for 11:30, he'd get me there at 12:15. If the rehearsal hall was available at ten, he'd lead me in around noon. David Winters and Mel Mandel finally had a talk with Chuck. They told him that unless I started making it to rehearsals, they'd have to take their names off the act.

This was the final straw, the ultimate indignity, and I found myself hating Chuck more than I ever had. He didn't care whether I ever learned how to sing or dance. He cared about only two things, the steady streams of money and sex that came to him because he was married to Linda Lovelace.

Maybe my pathetic little career was doomed from the start. Here I was, going on a stage, and I had never even seen a live play. I was going to be dancing in front of people, and I had never seen a professional dancer. Of course I was going to make a fool of myself. A fool twice over. I was already a fool to think Chuck would ever let me do anything on my own.

On the day I finally ran away from Chuck, he was particularly angry with me. All that morning he had yelled and screamed at me. Then, while I was rehearsing, he came barging into the rehearsal hall and told me he was calling off my work for the rest of the day.

"No!" I screamed right back at him. "I'm not going. This rehearsal is too important to me. You can go back to the office until I'm finished here and then you can come and get me."

"And when the fuck is that supposed to be?"

"Four-thirty!" I said. "That's supposed to be four-thirty!"

While Chuck and I were going at each other, the rest of the company stood silently by. They were all frightened of him. The week before they had seen him at his worst; he had hit me in front of everyone. Later David Winters and Mel Mandel spoke to Chuck alone and told him they would have to leave the act if that happened again. That conversation was still fresh in Chuck's mind.

"I'm supposed to leave you here until four-fucking-thirty?" he said.

"That's right!" I was still excited. "Just leave me alone!"

And he left. Chuck Traynor actually left. For once in my life, I had the last word in an argument with Chuck. But only God knows how determined I was that day. What

Chuck had been doing to me then made me angrier than all the things he had done before. It was one thing to force me to do indecent things; it was another to stand in the way of all my hopes for a decent life. When he left me alone that day, I threw myself into the rehearsals—really singing, really dancing, really feeling it. *I was into it.* For once I was into something with every part of me. The people there all saw the change.

"You know something, Linda?" one of the back-up dancers said. "This is the first time I've ever seen you smile."

"Oh, you've seen me smile."

"Just with your lips," he said.

"You know what it is," another dancer said. "This is the first time I've seen you when you looked like you were really living."

It was then that our writer, Mel Mandel, said something that changed my life. Maybe it was not all that profound or original, but it triggered something deep inside of me, and I've never forgotten it. At the moment he said it, it seemed to be a capsule holding all the truth in the world.

"I think I'd rather be dead," he said, "than not really be living."

I went back to my singing then but I couldn't get that thought out of my mind. All my energies during the past couple of years had gone toward preserving my life. I had stayed alive—but I had not really been living. And I agreed with Mel. Yes, it would be better to be dead than not really be living.

Later in the day, Chuck called to say that he was going to come to get me. For the second time in a single day, I told him no, that I needed more time for working. But what I really needed was more time for thinking.

By this time, David and Mel and most of the others had gone. The only one left with me was my choreographer and dance coach, Joe Cassini. Often, Joe and I would be the last ones in the rehearsal hall. I suddenly turned to him.

"Joe, could you drop me off somewhere?"

"But Chuck—"

"I don't want to be here when Chuck gets here," I said. "I don't ever want to be with Chuck again."

Joe was scared to death of Chuck and didn't try to hide that fact. Everyone who had ever seen Chuck's temper was scared of him.

"I won't tell Chuck who took me," I said. "But Joe, if you don't drive me away from here, I'm just going to start running. And I won't have a prayer. Chuck would find me and kill me. You know Chuck."

"Where could I take you?"

"The Beverly Hills Hotel."

I don't know why I chose a celebrity hangout like the Beverly Hills Hotel, or why I put my trust in a choreographer I barely knew, or why I signed the name "Linda Hyatt" when I registered, or why I did almost anything I was doing. But God was with me. God was definitely with me. No one at the hotel gave me a second glance, and no one recognized me as I went to my room. The bellboy left—"We hope you'll enjoy your stay with us, Miss Hyatt"—and I closed the door and locked it; then I took a deep breath.

Finally. Finally I was safe behind a locked door and the madman who ruled my life was on the other side of the city. My mind raced over everything that had gone down. Had I been too careless? Too trusting? Too stupid? No, I was all alone and Chuck Traynor had no way of finding me. I was accountable to no one, owned by no one.

It was a heady feeling and I gave in to it completely. One of the first things I did in that hotel room is the same gesture that millions of adolescents have done to declare their independence. I lit up a cigarette. I took in a deep swallow of the smoke and let it filter out through my nostrils. Today, years later, I'm still smoking. I know it's stupid and I intend to quit someday, but it will be on a day that I choose.

Then, a long hot tub bath. From time to time, I thought of Chuck—I imagined him furious and frantic, scurrying everywhere looking for me—and then I put him out of my mind. I thought about my past escape attempts and where they had gone wrong. They had failed because I had relied on other people, because I had gone to other people and sought help. Well, this time I was alone. I was relying on the strength of just one person, and I had no doubts about that person.

Later, relaxed from the bath and lying down, I finally got around to calling the offices of Linda Lovelace Enterprises. If Chuck had answered, I would have hung up the phone. But it was Dolores.

"Where *are* you?" she asked. "How *could* you leave me alone with that nut?"

"I better not tell you yet," I said. "It would only cause trouble for you. What's been happening?"

Dolores lowered her voice and talked rapidly. She said that Chuck was going berserk. He had called every taxi company in town and none of them would say they had picked me up. Then he had gotten hold of my co-workers— David Winters, Mel Mandel and even poor Joe Cassini— and he had ranted and raved at them. The latest thing he had done was to pack a loaded revolver in his flight bag and—

Suddenly Chuck was on the phone.

"Where in the fucking hell are you?" He was screaming. "What in the fuck do you think you're doing? Do you realize we're supposed to be meeting with Brodsky and his—"

I looked at that noisy little telephone receiver and dropped it into its cradle. *Click*. That simple. *Click,* and all that awful hysteria came to an end. It was such a pleasure being able to turn Chuck off, to sever his grip on me. And now he couldn't threaten me or yell at me or do anything to me at all. I reached for another cigarette.

The next time I spoke to Dolores was that evening and she was at her home.

"Linda, you must be very careful," she said. "Chuck's

a madman. He's got his gun with him and he's cruising everywhere looking for you. He's been here three different times."

"He'll never find me," I said. "I'd tell you where I am but it really would put you in danger—"

"Don't tell me," she said. "I don't want to know. You can tell me when Chuck has cooled down."

That didn't happen quickly. During the next few days, Chuck became more and more frantic. The meeting with Brodsky—and that represented ten or fifteen thousand in cash—had to be postponed again and again.

Chuck was paying visits to everyone who had been involved in the act with me. No longer was he alone. Now he was in the company of Vinnie, Lou Perry's old bodyguard. Somehow Chuck had persuaded Lou that I was being held against my will, that I had been kidnapped.

Chuck was very direct in talking to David Winters and Mel Mandel and the rest. If they tried to hide me or help me, he would kill them. He would also kill their wives and children. The threats became so bad that several of them got a court order barring Chuck Traynor from ever talking to them.

This time I was determined not to crack. Every day away from Chuck made me stronger, made it less possible that I would ever again go back to him. I didn't tell Dolores where I was until it was absolutely necessary and it was then that she proved herself to be a friend in need.

It was Dolores who advised me to move out of the Beverly Hills Hotel; there were too many people who might recognize me there. It was Dolores who drew some cash out of the company for me; Dolores who showed up with wigs and new clothes; Dolores who checked me out of the hotel and then drove me to a new hotel while I crouched on the floor of her car. And it was Dolores who arranged for two bodyguards to watch over me twenty-four hours a day.

In the company of one of the bodyguards, Dolores and I took a wild chance and drove out to the Malibu cottage Chuck and I had been renting. We went frantically through bureaus and closets, grabbing everything we could get our hands on and taking it out to the car. After a short time of this, the bodyguard became suspicious.

"Hey, what's going on here?" he said. "Are you two girls doing something you're not supposed to do?"

While I was hiding out, my brand new career as a stage performer came to an end. The men who had been working with me explained that they enjoyed working with me but they also enjoyed breathing; Chuck had told them they couldn't have it both ways.

As the days went on, my only constant companion was fear. Every time I spoke to Dolores, she had a new story about Chuck, a new threat or a new tantrum. There was no longer any question about going back to Chuck. The other times I had tried to escape, the punishment had been unbearable. This time he would surely kill me. So be it. This time he would *have* to kill me. This time I would choose death ahead of Chuck Traynor. I kept thinking about what Mel Mandel had said that day: *I'd rather be dead than not really be living*.

While I was alone, with plenty of time to think, I asked myself why I hadn't taken this step before. Why hadn't I made the complete break? The answer: I was not strong enough. I was the kind of person who needed to draw strength from other people. The people I met with Chuck were not the kind of people anyone could draw strength from; they had no strength to spare.

Finally I had been exposed to decent people with talent. I became stronger by seeing myself through their eyes—I was not crazy, not sick, not a bad person. They had made me feel like a whole human being again and so I had finally been able to function as a human being.

I needed strength now more than ever. I learned that Chuck was searching for me with both his pistol and his automatic rifle by his side. Acting on Dolores' suggestion, I called the police. They knew who I was and they listened to my story about my husband coming after me with a gun. I gave up forever on police help when I was told, "Lady, we can't get involved in domestic affairs."

While I was still hiding out, I called Sammy Davis, Jr. This time I told him everything, my true feelings about everything. I know now that I was looking for more support, perhaps even for a place to go. What I got instead was a little philosophy.

"Well," he said, "you've got to do what you've got to do."

I'm sure that meant something very profound. But what it meant to me was that I was on my own. I guess I already knew that. Everyone has to learn that sometime, but it's still a hard lesson. I was on my own and I would just have to wait Chuck out.

Basically that's what happened. He finally stopped threatening to kill everyone. Now he began the bargaining and the wheedling. He would change his ways; he would help me with my career; he would do anything if I agreed to come back to him.

Messages went back and forth. Now Chuck was desperate. He could see our backer, Gerry Brodsky, and all his cash, disappearing from sight. And all those deals were going down the toilet where most of them belonged. Now he was saying that I didn't have to live with him; it would be enough to just *pretend* long enough to get the rest of the money from Brodsky. The message went back to him that I wanted to have my own lawyer for any new deals. The message came back to me that he wanted one last chance to talk to me.

I agreed to a telephone call. I tape-recorded that call. Chuck began by saying that it was now or never; if we didn't land Brodsky now, the big fish would get away from us. I insisted that I wanted a lawyer, and I meant my own real lawyer, not Philip Mandina.

"What can I do, man?" Chuck said. "What'm I gonna

say? Maybe if Brodsky sees us both smiling at each other, he'll calm down a little bit. He's seen us fight and that was a mistake. I told you not to fuck around but you can't listen—"

"Well, if everything is the way you say it is, what difference does it make if an attorney looks at it?"

"I don't want *my* wife to have an attorney, it's that simple."

"Why not?"

"Because it's bullshit," he said. "You're my wife. I'm your husband. We are married. And *we* have *our* attorney. And if you got an attorney on your own, it's only for one fucking reason. It's to file for a fucking divorce or to set things up for our Linda's private fucking deals. That I will not go along with. I'm very sorry, but you *are* my wife. I love you. I take care of you."

*I take care of you*—I almost laughed at that. Throughout this, our last conversation, I had the feeling that Chuck was divided and in turmoil with himself. At times he seemed to be reading a script prepared by a lawyer; at other times it was pure Chuck Traynor.

"I mean, if you're this alien to me," he was saying, "you—you're talking to me like I'm a total fucking stranger, like I'm some god-damned rip-off artist who's trying to fucking take you over the coals. I'm not going to take that, honey. You're my wife. And I love you. But I won't take this kind of shit. Now you know, you've pushed and pushed, and I've backed and backed. I'm not backing any farther. I want this show to go on. But I won't take this kind of shit. All I want is to put us back together. You can start with your rehearsals. And spend as much time as you can in putting us back together—without interfering with your rehearsals.

"But there'll be . . . no . . . fucking . . . attorney . . . around. You and your husband have an attorney. His name is Philip J. Mandina. He is *our* attorney. If Miss Linda Lovelace has an attorney, I don't want to know nothing

about it. 'Cause that's bullshit. There is no Miss Linda Lovelace. You are Missus Charles Traynor. And *Mister* Charles
Traynor takes care of Missus Charles Traynor.

"So, listen, man, knock it off! *Now!* While we still got
something we can put back together. You're gonna take
about one more step, babe, and there ain't gonna be nothing
to put back together."

"Well, first of all, that's what *you* want," I said, finally
breaking into his monologue. "That's what you say and
that's fine for you."

"Look, I love you and you are my wife," he said. "I do
not think you have sufficient reason to stay separated from
me. I think what you are doing is a bullshit deal. You know,
I was kind enough—and *am* kind enough—to put up with it
for a little bit. I have not given you grounds to stop loving
me. And you better not fucking act like I fucking have.
Cause I have *not*. I have done nothing wrong. If you go
to court with me, you're going to look like a complete asshole. I haven't fucking run out on you. I don't drink. I
supported you well. I've taken care of you."

*Taken care of me . . . supported me . . . loved me*—from
then to the end of the conversation, I didn't say a single
word. It didn't matter. Chuck was off now. And in his final
speech to me I can hear his world come crashing down
around him. He was losing his meal ticket and his sex ticket
and there was absolutely no mistaking the panic in his
voice.

"You see, Linda," he was saying, "there's nothing for you
to sign. All you got to do is stick out your hand, take a
piece of paper and watch me sign a contract. You're not
going to sign anything. And there's no way you can get
fucked. I can go over there and sign the contract without
you. Except without you and I going in, and being ourselves,
husband and wife, Brodsky isn't going to put up the money.
And if Brodsky doesn't put up the money, Linda, we're
*done!* Don't you understand that? *Done!*

"We got twenty thousand left in the bank. And about five

thousand we're going to owe David Winters because there's fifteen thousand on the contract and he's got five more coming. We're gonna end up with like eight thousand dollars to divide between us for our divorce. And your attorney will take a third of yours. That's really a nice way to go, isn't it?

"We were close to becoming millionaires. You know? And if you don't want nothing else, just fake it, Babe. But don't pull this shit. Because this shit won't work. You know, if you hate my guts, fine. Sleep in the next room. You know, I can feel the same way about you that you feel about me, whether it's good or bad. But don't fucking blow the whole business. We've worked for four fucking years to get here. We're right on the doorstep now. But one fucking move by you and it's *gone!*

"Now you got nothing to lose, Babe. Nothing. You have signed all the papers that you have already signed. That fucking attorney can't erase the contracts that you signed, can't erase anything. I can give you half the company. You don't have to sign anything, you don't have to do anything. You just have to take it in your fucking hands. You just have to sit there with a grin on your face while I sign the fucking contract. It may be distasteful but you could smile at me or maybe kiss me, just once, so Brodsky will feel cool, like we're ironing this thing out, you know.

"I mean, what the fuck? You know? Man, you're thinking crazy, and you better get your shit back together. I mean, you better be thinking about a rehearsal, not this legal shit, not this, 'I don't think we're getting back together.' If we're not going back together, then fuck it! Let's end up with $8,000 and divide it in half and get a fucking divorce. I'm not going around and making more of an ass out of myself than I already done.

"Whatshisname, the guy from Head Shampoo, he's not gonna sign any contract. The contract he's got is with Linda Lovelace Enterprises. *I'm* the President. He wants you to endorse his product; he wants me to sign the contract. If I tell him we're split up, what the fuck you think he's gonna

do? Think he's gonna give twenty-five grand? Shit, no! Now
. . . knock . . . it . . . off, Linda. Get your ass into fucking
gear. Get over here! Get dressed! We'll go over to Brodsky's.
Now we can do that and things'll be cool. Don't do that
and things aren't gonna be cool.

"Man, you're going down the wrong road, Linda. I'm
telling you. I'm your old man. And I love you. Now knock
off this fucking shit and get back over here where you're
supposed to be and take your stock certificate. You got 50
percent of *our* company. And if you just put an honest
effort in putting you and I back together, that's what I
want in exchange for what I'm gonna do. Man, that's all I
ask. If I'm asking too much, then fuck it."

I hung up the telephone.

# *twenty*

One night David Winters invited me out for dinner and a talk, a memorial service for my poor dead act. We picked Alice's Restaurant because we knew it would be the kind of restaurant Chuck would never choose. We walked in the front door and I froze. The first person I saw in the restaurant was Chuck Traynor. In that same glance, I saw that he had his little gun bag resting by his feet.

Sitting across the table from Chuck was a new porno queen, Marilyn Chambers, the former Ivory Snow girl who had starred in *Behind the Green Door*. While I'd still been with Chuck, he had contacted Marilyn Chambers to see whether they couldn't be involved in projects together. Since then, I've read that Chuck is her business manager and that they've gotten married; I hope both arrangements work out better for her than they did for me.

The pressure from Chuck remained intense. And everywhere he went in his search for me, he was accompanied by Lou Perry's man, Vinnie. Through a mutual friend, I finally reached Lou and asked him why he was letting Chuck use Vinnie. Lou had been told that I was forcibly taken from Chuck and was being held against my will. And he was simply avenging a *paisano*'s honor; despite everything he knew about my life with Chuck, Lou saw this as protection of hearth and home. When he learned the true story, Vinnie was called back from the front lines.

And then it stopped.

It all just stopped.

It ended. Just like that. Just that quickly. I don't know why. One day I was hiding under wigs and sunglasses and sneaking around corners. The next day I heard through my new attorney that Chuck Traynor was prepared to sign a divorce agreement.

Why? Was Marilyn Chambers now occupying his full attention? Did Lou Perry order him to cease and desist? Did he lose heart when people took out court orders against him? It's impossible to tell you what was going on in Chuck's mind; I could never tell that when I was with him.

And that really didn't matter. All that mattered was that I was finally going to be free of Chuck Traynor. Chuck would be off my case forever. And using a new attorney, we worked out a division of all our worldly goods. We divided them after marriage much as we divided them during marriage. Chuck took the Jaguar, the motorcycle, the couch, two tables, a stereo, a color television, wall fixtures, barrel chairs, binoculars, camera, movie camera, hammocks and cushions. Total value: $12,000. I took a bed, a dresser, a radio, two speakers, a tape deck, a cassette deck, a turntable, an amplifier and a slide projector. Total value: $1,500.

But there was one possession not included in the list. Me. One human being, misused, and badly scarred, but young and strong and anxious to live a life. Total value: still undetermined.

When signing the divorce agreement, I met Chuck one last time. We shared an elevator on our way to the lawyer's office. I was surprised that he no longer generated fear. He seemed innocuous, a balding middle-aged man with a Fu Manchu mustache. I'll never forget his parting words.

"Just remember that I love you," he said. "And if you ever change your mind, I'll always be there."

I'm sure that's the truth. Chuck Traynor always will be there. I'm aware that he is out there somewhere, and every now and then, he makes a guest appearance in my nightmares. And at odd times, when I least expect it, I'll see him in the face of a stranger coming down the street toward me. Or I'll be talking to someone and I'll see him in the eyes or the smile or just a gesture. He is there and he always will be there.

My little stage act had died at birth. But out of the ashes, new life. I became friends, then lovers, with David Winters.

Every woman should know a David Winters at least once in her life. A David Winters who brings fresh roses every day and offers them with a sweeping bow. A David Winters who races to open a door or light a cigarette or throw a kiss. I've always been an incurable romantic and David Winters could have been designed in my daydreams, seemingly the exact opposite of Chuck. If he never did anything else on God's earth, David Winters did one thing: He helped me get back the self-respect that Chuck had stolen.

Money never mattered to David. Not in the least. When I first knew him, he told me that he was six million dollars in debt and going through bankruptcy. But little details like that didn't even slow him down.

"Six-*million* dollars?" I said. "How can that be?"

I soon found out how that can be. Shopping became a way of life for us. He insisted that we go to the best stores in Beverly Hills. I no longer bought one pair of boots; I ordered a dozen of them. And why buy a gown in white when it was also available in a rainbow of colors? When I decided to get a car, David recommended a Bentley.

"Isn't that expensive?" I said.

"Not in the long run," he explained to me. "You've been in serious accidents. If you had been driving a Bentley, you'd have come through without a scratch."

I may be one of the only people on earth to get a Bentley

for safety reasons. But there's no doubt that it was an extravagance. I could have been just as happy with a Mercedes. I have to laugh at that thought; you should see the ten-year-old heap I'm driving these days. I'm lucky if it makes it to the corner deli without a mechanical breakdown.

And that was not just a matter of gestures; that was the way he was with me. He asked my opinions about everything. He allowed his eyes to light up when he saw me. He persuaded me that I was not a freak, not an ugly, worthless piece of garbage. And he also happened to be the first adult male I knew well who was not a pervert.

From the beginning, we shared tenderness and warmth. I clung to him the way a drowning person would hang onto a life preserver, the way a poisoned man would reach for an antidote. For the first time in my life, I fell in love. David brought up tender feelings and emotions that I didn't know I had. And I'll always feel, no matter what happened to us, that I was blessed to have a David Winters enter my life after a Chuck Traynor.

David's special talent was beauty. He had a genius for beauty. He had worked on stage and in films with the world's most beautiful women and somehow he had made them even more beautiful. I believe he could take a Phyllis Diller and she would become gentle and soft-spoken and sensuous. He even made me feel beautiful. And you know something? When you feel beautiful, you *become* beautiful. I *was* beautiful.

But that's the point. Life with David Winters was a fantasy, a bubble, a fairy tale complete with handsome princes and shiny limousines. It was false fingernails and Gene Shacove doing my hair. It was a trip to the Cannes film festival and a sudden flight to Paris for dinner, this because a girl should not go through life without having had dinner in Paris at least once. It was a long-stemmed rose on a pillow. It was a thousand-dollar-a-month beach cottage. It was high-fashion photographs by Milton Greene and dozens of gowns and a sable coat and all the beautiful things on earth.

If I had any complaints about David then—and, believe me, I didn't—they would have been about his love affair with the telephone. David was born with a telephone in his ear. He carried on telephone calls from swimming pools and bathtubs. If he had no plans on a particular day, he would take out his personal bible—his phone book—and work his way from A to Z, calling everyone who had ever meant anything to him.

In retrospect, I would have just two words of advice to anyone leading the kind of life I was leading with David Winters: bring money. Lots of money. Not that we let the thought of money interfere with our happiness. We didn't. In fact, we didn't even carry money with us. We signed my name to everything. I look at my diary and day after day there is a single notation: "Shopping" or "Shopping again today."

And, of course, there was no need to cook our own food, not with all those lovely restaurants. And all they ever required was my signature. My signature worked for David's mortgage and his gardener, for car payments and meals, for everything. In just three months, using two credit cards, I ran up tabs of $25,000.

But that didn't disturb me. Not only was David Winters loving me, he was putting together a whole new career for me. A legitimate career. You'd be surprised how much money is needed to launch a legitimate career. But who was counting? What person in love ever stopped to figure out the tab? I had never seen any money in the past and it didn't seem all that important now.

And what could money matter when David was there, bringing me a new gift every day? A bouquet of flowers. A book of love poems. Or just a card with a pretty thought written on it.

I have to admit that I've never been any good with money.

Even after I got high-priced accountants—no, *especially* after I got high-priced accountants—I never knew how much money I had or where it was. With Chuck out of my life, I wanted to trust people. I still have that desire. If I ever become too skeptical, or too cynical, I won't survive. I just have to forget everything that ever happened to me and look on each new person as a good human being.

There was no way to put my stage act together again, not after Chuck threatened to kill anyone who helped me. And when I was unable to make the November first date in Miami, it cost me $30,000. You see, I was sued by Chuck's Florida lawyer, Philip J. Mandina, for breaking my contract. He got approximately $20,000 in a settlement, and the Florida lawyers defending me got $10,000 in fees.

But it was only $30,000; that's what my new advisers told me. Only $30,000. I was told not to worry about that because a fantastic new career was about to open up for me. A legitimate career.

There was the wonderful world of television, for example. They were about to film a new adult series called *Soap* and I would be a natural for that. Someone involved with *Movie of the Week* was interested in me. Writers, directors, and producers were all coming to us with projects and proposals, straight non-pornographic projects and proposals. But evidently the studio heads and network executives took a secret vote and decided that I must not be allowed to corrupt the morals of the nation. And you know something? I have never appeared in a network television production. Never once. And I suppose the nation's morals have gone uncorrupted.

Oh, there was work available. Porno work. If I wanted to star in another freak show, there would be plenty of work for me to do. And money, plenty of money.

My feeling about those offers was simple: no. I will never do anything pornographic again.

I look at my life then and I know I went along with some things. I was wearing revealing clothes and signing autographs and enjoying the attention that came my way. But I wasn't being dirty. I wasn't being thrown into a room with five men. I was wearing silk and satin, and, if I was in a room with men, it was to discuss a contract or a deal, not their favorite perversions. Most of the propositions I was listening to were clean ones.

Maybe at times I did get a little carried away with myself, a little impressed by the fact that I was Linda Lovelace, but I always came back down to earth. When we were in France for the Cannes film festival, I was walking into a hotel lobby as the famous actor Rex Harrison was walking out. When he recognized me, a fantastic smile creased those famous features and he called out to me, "Miss Lovelace, I *must* shake your hand." *Rex Harrison!* I was so pleased and flattered. Then later I had time to think about it. Hey, wait a minute. I hadn't just done a great film that had gotten me an Academy Award. I had been in a disgusting film with disgusting people. All those celebrities who wanted to meet me—what were they doing watching a movie like that in the first place?

The offers coming our way were varied: tee-shirts, posters, record albums, commercials, books, college lectures, public appearances at car-racing tracks, pornographic cassettes. In a way, the proposals were like ghosts—they loomed large for a brief moment, then disappeared without ever quite materializing.

Since I was now able to meet the press on my own, without Chuck feeding me lines, I decided to tell the truth. And I did. I told the exact story you've been reading here—that I had been brutalized, raped and forced into every sexual situation imaginable. But maybe you never read that story in your favorite tabloid. They couldn't use that story. The minute I started telling it, the reporters would turn off their tape recorders. They'd explain to me about the laws of libel. And then they'd point out that the true story would really be a downer for their readers.

Finally, since the truth got such a negative reaction from

everyone, I was advised to become more general in my answers and to talk about my present, not my past. Unfortunately, my present wasn't much to talk about. My only stage appearance was in a sex farce, *Pajama Tops*, that closed during the first week of its run in Philadelphia. There were no decent movie offers. And the only apparent way to make money was to go back and do a second book.

This time I was looking forward to the thought of doing a book. This time I would be free to tell the truth. And my writer this time would be Mel Mandel, a man who not only knew the true story but who had lived some of it with me. And so Mel tape-recorded my memories of life with Chuck and sat down to write *The Intimate Diary of Linda Lovelace*.

Well, life is filled with hard lessons. And the lesson I learned this time is that no one really wants to hear the truth. The publisher read the manuscript and was deeply disturbed to realize that it was not another *Inside Linda Lovelace*. They complained that there wasn't enough sex; they said they couldn't publish it in its present condition. It was explained to me that what really happened wasn't important; what people *thought* had happened—that was important.

David Winters thought the situation over and said that we should give the publishers what they wanted.

"We'll try a little bit of the truth now," he said. "Then, later on, a little more of the truth. Anyway, the world wouldn't accept it; no one would believe it if you told the whole truth all at once."

So David and Mel got together and made up the stuff that the publisher wanted in the book. The big difference between the two books is that in the second one, Chuck is described as a villain. No longer is he the world's greatest lover. No, now the world's greatest lover is David Winters.

*With a tremendous thrust, he put that surging, gorgeous cock inside me. A pulsating jackhammer that kept driving, driving, driving, plowing into me, over and over.*

Trash.

Then they made up a lot of other things that had nothing at all to do with real life. They wrote about my desire for other women and my skill with vibrators. Trash and garbage, all trash and garbage. I didn't blame Mel Mandel when he put a make-believe name on the book ("as told to Carl Wallin"); I wish they'd never used my name either.

I never realized how many lies you have to tell to sell a book. They invented a sex scene with a father and a son, both supposed to be famous Hollywood actors. And another scene between me and a telephone repairman. Then they added one with a famous football player that they wanted everyone to think was Joe Namath. All trash and garbage.

The truth of the matter was that I did meet Joe Namath at a party. I went over to the world-famous football player and introduced myself. He suddenly saw a young chick on the other side of the room and he said, "Oh, excuse me," and then he was gone. That's the whole story, the true story of my intimate life with Joe Namath, but I guess that wouldn't have sold too many books.

They managed to get a quote from Hefner for the cover of the book: "Linda is the new sex goddess of the 70s!" And they added a centerfold, a bunch of revealing photographs, and they shipped it out.

That whole book was make-believe, no better than the first one. Maybe that makes it a good California book. Because so much of life out there is make-believe. It's all cocktail-party talk, deals that vanish, and early enthusiasms that fade away—all smoke and fantasy.

Sometimes I wonder what kind of person would read a book like that one and what would he think? It's completely schized out. Half of the book is complaining about all the terrible things I was forced to do. The other half says how much I love doing all those terrible things. In publishing, I guess they figure that half a truth is better than no truth at all. To me, it's still a lie.

Finally David Winters and Mel Mandel found a movie I could do. It began its life as a proposed comedy album— *Linda Lovelace for President*—and the idea became a movie.

But not the kind of movie I had done in the past. Oh, no, not that! This was going to be a really first-rate comedy, the kind of picture that Carole Lombard once did. Top comedy writers, men like Chuck McCann, were going to be consultants. The producer-director was Arthur Marks, a man involved with putting the *Perry Mason* shows on television. And my salary was going to be a payment of $25,000 against a percentage of the profits.

Before signing the contract, David and I went over every detail of the movie with Arthur Marks. The sex issue came up during our first discussion and it was settled at once.

"How far will you go?" I was asked. "Will you do soft-core sex scenes?"

"No."

"She's not doing anything like that any more," David spoke up. "Never again."

"Fine. Now, just let me know this: nudity or no? We get the nudity business cleared up now, there'll be no hassles later on."

"No nudity," I said.

"Fine," I was told. "No problem."

So we were going to make a big color comedy about a certain Linda Lovelace running for the office of President of the United States. Without nudity and without sex, but with all the comic talent that money could buy. Not only was I signed as the star of the movie, David was signed to be co-producer.

I see now that something was going on between David and myself. Or maybe something was not going on. Whatever, we weren't as close emotionally as we had once been. Most evenings we found ourselves going over to the Playboy mansion where David would play backgammon. That way we didn't have to talk much. Things weren't perfect. But

I didn't realize how far apart we really were until we started making the movie.

From the first day of shooting, I realized the movie was dumb. One of the dumbest movies ever made. None of that high-priced talent ever showed up. The script was something you laughed at, not with. But at least nothing dirty was coming down. At first.

Then one morning we had finished shooting and were sitting down for lunch. Director Arthur Marks came over to us.

"Okay, Linda," he said, "get ready for the fuck-and-suck scenes."

*"What?"*

I waited for David Winters to stand up and defend me against this idiotic suggestion. I could almost hear him say, "Mr. Marks, what are you talking about?" Yes, I could *almost* hear him say that—almost but not quite, because David never said a word. The co-producer of the movie turned to me and shrugged his shoulders helplessly.

For about one second I was furious. Then disappointed. Then heartbroken. Then finished, just done in. I looked at this man who had made me feel like such a human being. For almost a year he had been my knight in shining armor, my slayer of California dragons, my last line of defense against the sharpies and the conmen and the sleaze artists. This was the same man who had called Chuck Traynor a complete degenerate. And now, in a single instant, he did a one-eighty, a total turn-around.

I ran from him toward my trailer. Dolores was there to comfort me, to listen as I said the same thing over and over again, "I can't believe it; I can't believe this is happening to me."

"Take it easy," Dolores told me. "Linda, you don't *have* to do it. You don't have to do anything you don't want to do, not ever again."

Oh, I needed to hear that. Especially when David came back to explain everything to me: I would only have to do it in *this* movie; they weren't going to show *everything*, not *all* the details; they were just going to show *part* of it.

This time I didn't go along with them. This time I refused. They went on shooting the movie, as I knew they would. And they went on calling it a "sex comedy" although they weren't supplying any comedy, and I wasn't supplying any sex.

The issue came up just one more time. We were in Kansas, filming on location. And again Arthur Marks came up to me.

"Linda, you'll have to take off your clothes for this next scene."

"I'm not taking my clothes off."

"You misunderstand me. I'm not asking you. I'm telling you to take off your clothes. We're doing the sex scenes next."

"Then do them without me. I'm not doing any sex scenes."

"You're fired."

"Good."

"You'll never work in movies again."

I walked off the set then and went back to my hotel room. I was sure they would come to their senses. But then the pressure started. From David, from my new lawyer, from accountants, from everyone. They kept telling me I would have to go along. If I didn't, I'd be guilty of walking off a set and I'd be blacklisted in the business. And they quoted from my contract. *Clause Four: Arthur Marks will supervise production and will exercise creative and artistic control of the film. Linda Lovelace will follow his direction.*

I hate to have to admit that I wound up compromising a little. No sex scenes. But some nudity.

As the movie was coming to an end, so were David Winters and myself. And it was not an easy end. It was, in fact, violent. He beat me up. But I don't want to go into the details here because that was just an incident, not typical of our year together. My love for David was a perfect bubble, but bubbles do burst.

# *twenty-one*

---

And then I met my husband. I'd rather not tell you his name because he's already gone through enough trouble. You'd be surprised how people react when they learn your wife was once a person named Linda Lovelace.

I thank God I was able to make love to my husband. After this whole ordeal, I found myself disliking all men on sight. I still distrust most men instinctively. It was a great surprise to learn there was one man I wanted to love, a man I could actually *enjoy* making love to. I still consider this a small miracle.

My husband is a strong man. He has had to be. The minute someone recognizes me or discovers who his wife is, the remarks begin. He also happens to be an old-fashioned man, the kind who believes you're supposed to defend your woman's honor. Defending the honor of a Linda Lovelace can be a full-time occupation.

My husband is someone I knew when we were both young. To him, I will always be the former Linda Boreman, *not* the former Linda Lovelace. We got together just as I was coming down from my year with David Winters. He saw me as a confused young woman wearing see-through blouses, trying to live the life of a Hollywood star. By this time I had learned how hard it was to escape my past. All my advisers were telling me that since I couldn't escape my past, I should make peace with it. Since everyone expected me to be a certain way, then that's the way I should be.

I didn't know what to do.

I needed to hear another voice, and that voice belonged to the man who was to become my husband and the father of our child. In the beginning, he volunteered to help me sort through the financial debris of my life, and I accepted that offer gratefully.

He went through all my records. Then he wrote down two long lists of numbers, added them up, compared them, stared at them in disbelief.

"How much money do I have?"

"Are you sure you want to know?"

"What's the bad news?"

"Well, Linda, it looks as though you owe about fifty thousand dollars."

"I *owe* fifty thousand?"

"Give or take a few thousand," he said. "A lot of money came in over the past couple of years but a lot more went out."

I had to go back to work so that's what I did. And whatever I did after this, whatever project I became involved in, it always seemed to be a replay of what had already come down.

Just one example. The people who had produced an enormously successful R-rated movie, *Emanuelle*, had been talking to me about starring in a movie called *Laurie*. The up-front money would be $50,000, enough to clean up my debts, and there would be more to follow. R-rated didn't sound good to me but it sounded better than X-rated.

And this time there would be no doubt, no confusion. My husband-to-be sat through the conferences and meetings.

All hard-core sex was out. Nudity was out. This time there was no doubt about it, no fuzzy areas.

Oh, this time I had high hopes. The script they showed me was about the size of an issue of *TV Guide*. It was a beautiful love story about a woman who was deeply in love with her husband and they share a great adventure. I was cast as an anthropologist studying the Maya Indians on a South Pacific island, Zamboanga.

However, by the time we got to Rome, the script had grown. Now it was as large as the Manhattan phone book. It went from a beautiful thing to pure sleaze. It had me going to bed with twelve different people, including one transvestite. It had me masturbating with camera lenses. Being with fags. Being with lesbians. *Yecccccchhhhhhh!*

I shouldn't have been surprised. It was simple type-casting. I had once been a sexual commodity, and that's what everyone wanted me to be forever. If I had started out as someone else—if I had begun as, say, an Elizabeth Taylor—no one would ever have asked me to do the things that everyone was now asking me to do. Nor would they take an Elizabeth Taylor from a movie like *National Velvet* and then ask her to make love to a camera lens.

When we got to Rome, I told them sorry but I wasn't going to do any of that stuff. Instead of rewriting the script, they moved me from a leading role to a lesser role. They hired another actress for the lead, someone more willing to follow their script. Now I found myself playing a pregnant woman who waves goodbye to her husband as he goes off to study the Mayas in Zamboanga.

For my husband-to-be, this was all an education. He had lived his life as a working man and he had no idea what kind of lives movie people led. He learned. He learned one night when we were invited to have dinner with the director and his wife. In their hotel room after dinner, the man started speaking.

"We must really get to know each other better," he said.

"All four of us. So that we can work better on the movie."

"That sounds like a good idea," I said.

"Yes, it is so important," he went on, "that we all be involved with each other . . . intimately."

"Really?"

"Yes, it is important that we learn how each of us touches and feels." He reached out and touched my hand, lightly. "If you know what I mean."

"Yes, I know just what you mean," I said. "But we're very tired now and must get some sleep."

Later, when I explained to my husband-to-be what was coming down, he was angry and offended. I told him this was the way that everyone in movies behaved; this was the way they *were*. He couldn't believe me then, but he believes me now.

Then we were given still other script changes. Now cast as the pregnant wife, I suddenly found myself locked in a room with two homosexuals, saying the most idiotic things imaginable. I wrote the director a short note complaining about the changes and saying that his writing talent seemed to be suffering in the tropical heat. He fired me on the spot, and we caught the next plane back to the States.

# twenty-two

That was the end, my last picture show, the final starring role for Linda Lovelace. There would be another venture, a deservedly short-lived sex farce in Las Vegas, something called *My Daughter's Rated X*. And then, nothing.

Oh, other movies were offered to me, are still offered to me, but there is always a catch. Always *the* catch.

The patterns didn't change. I would go into a big office, and men wearing business suits and ties would treat me with respect. They would describe their new movie project and it would sound like a beautiful love story or a screamingly funny comedy. There would be meeting after meeting. The ties would come off and the collars would be loosened. At each meeting the story would change slightly. All of a sudden there would be a nude scene, then another. And a sex scene. Soft-core, of course. Then hard-core, maybe just one hard-core scene. Or two. And by the time anyone ever saw a movie camera, we'd all be knee-deep in garbage. And somewhere along the line I'd have to tell the men in their business suits to take a hike.

There were other propositions, as well. The possible

three-picture contract if I would just give so-and-so a sample of my wares. The network show if I'd go to bed with Mister Big. The comedy that would be written just after I deep-throated the director.

It's all such a shame. Because I would have *loved* being an actress. This was something I dreamed about when I was a little girl. But I wanted to be an actress the way Susan Hayward was an actress. And that was never to be.

Regrets? Many. Once, just once in my life, I would have enjoyed being in a movie where there was a real story and a real script. A movie where actors had to memorize lines. A movie where the director would say something like, "Let me tell you what your motivation is going to be in this next scene." A movie where you felt they had film in the camera. A movie where you didn't have to do anything disgusting.

The funny thing is that I would really have enjoyed being a regular actress. Because I'm good at it. I know I could have done it. I still have a fantasy of making one movie, one decent movie, and winning an Academy Award and having all those people knocking at my door so that I could say to them, "I'm sorry—you're too late. You should have been there when I needed you."

The last movie offer I heard about, one that was presented to a lawyer, was for a huge sum of money. I'm talking about more than a million dollars. All I had to do was make one more pornographic movie, just one more *Deep Throat*. The money was to be deposited in a Swiss bank account before the first day of filming.

Well, I refused to do it then, and I refuse to do it now. I mean, give me one million dollars or give me fifty million and I still won't do it. And that's that.

Every now and then I'll pick up a newspaper and see that a new X-rated movie is opening and it "stars Linda Love-lace." Don't ever believe it. All that means is that they are including a scene from *Deep Throat*. I never made another dirty movie and I never will.

Nothing much has really changed. Chuck Traynor is back at the same old stand, managing the career of Marilyn Chambers. In a recent interview he talked about me and he said, "She was better at housework and cooking than sex. She was a lousy lover. When I first dated her, she was so shy it shocked her to be seen in the nude by a man." I consider that the first honest thing Chuck ever said about me. I sometimes wonder how he'll react to this book, how he'll feel when the truth is there for everyone to read. I think he'll look on this as an advertisement, a way of reaching more freaks.

Sometimes I look back and I laugh. Thank God I can still laugh. I remember how I was living after getting rid of Chuck. I'd go to a new hotel and as I was checking in, I'd tell room service to bring me a cold platter of lobster and shrimp and plenty of champagne on ice. Not just any champagne, mind you. It had to be Mumm's. If they only had Dom Perignon, I wasn't interested.

I think about that and I have to laugh. These days I can't afford to buy a bottle of California wine or a single shrimp. I have felt real poverty these past few years, and I've been on welfare. I feel poverty very intensely. I've gotten so I hate the last few days of the month when there is no food in the house.

I just hope that when this book comes out, I'm not on welfare. That would be embarrassing. It's terrible never being able to get in the car and just go for a ride; first we have to make sure that we have enough gas to go back and forth. And I always have to make sure that I have a dime for a phone call, in case there's an emergency.

I hope this book brings us some money. In a way, it's an interesting experiment. The other books, the trash and the garbage, made a lot of money. What will the truth do? Was the other publisher right when he said that no one wanted to read the truth?

This time if there is any money, it won't just vanish. It

will go right into a trust fund. The one thing I want someday is a home, just a small home. And, if it were possible,
I'd like to buy one of those little foreign cars, forty miles
to the gallon. I'd like someday to live in peace and quiet,
with my husband able to go out and work for a living. I
would like one more baby, a girl, and I would like a garden
of my own.

Why haven't I done these things already? Because it's one
thing to be Linda Lovelace with plenty of money and
round-the-clock bodyguards. It's another thing to be Linda
Lovelace with no money, with an infant son, and with no
protection. Once I'm identified, our life falls apart. My
husband has to leave his job to protect us and to move us
somewhere else. Where I'm recognized again and again,
I'm the target of freaks and degenerates.

When I was with Chuck, I was sure he had to be one of
a kind. There could be no one else on earth like that. Now
I know better. There are Chucks everywhere and there is
some of Chuck in many people. I see it even in people who
were once good friends of mine, people in their twenties
and early thirties. Suddenly they're swapping mates and
having affairs with each other's wives and going to sex
clubs. I don't understand these people at all. I don't understand America anymore.

Thank God I love my husband. Thank God we can have
a normal, healthy, and happy love life. I really do thank God
for this. But my husband has been good to me and he's not
sick like those other people. Everyone I met out in California seemed to have the sickness. California is really bad.
Worse, I think, than any place else. But I don't know for
sure; it's all around, everywhere.

How can you identify a Chuck Traynor? The answer: you
can't. At first Chuck seemed normal and nice. Suddenly there
was a gun in his hand and it was pointed at my head. I never
thought something like that could happen to me, but now I
know better. It could happen to me, and it could happen to
you.

This story is not unique. There are plenty of Chuck Traynors out there. And an endless supply of girls who are young, trusting, gullible, and sometimes a little stupid. And it is certain that these people will, from time to time, come together. By the time they are pried apart, incredible damage can be done.

# *epilogue*

All this seems far away. Today, after finishing this, I'm going to clean my house. I've borrowed a vacuum cleaner for the afternoon and the thought of doing that gives me a great deal of pleasure. I'm a cleanliness nut, and if my little house isn't spotless, I get very upset.

My vices aren't much to talk about these days. When we can afford it, I like nothing better than a beer while I'm watching a football game on television. Sometimes I think I'll drive my husband nuts, the way I like sports.

I'm not so hard on myself these days. Maybe it's because I'm so busy taking care of a three-year-old son, a husband, a house, and two cats. I look back at Linda Lovelace and I understand her; I know why she did what she did. It was because she felt it was better to live than to die.

Sure, I could have *not* done a lot of things. But I would have been dead. Or my parents would have been dead. And I didn't want anyone to die. I knew that God would one day show me the way to get away from Traynor. And that's what kept me going and accepting all the things that had happened. I just put my faith in God and got through it.